THE
FORGIVENESS
PROJECT

Is there a relationship between forgiveness and cancer? Based upon his years of experience in working with cancer patients, Dr. Barry seeks to answer this very important question. His conclusions are based upon credible research, and have proven to be helpful to his patients and others. This book raises the discussion of forgiveness to a new and higher level. I recommend *The Forgiveness Project* to anyone struggling to find forgiveness.

Harold G. Koenig, MD
Professor of Psychiatry & Behavioral Sciences
Associate Professor of Medicine
Director, Center for Spirituality, Theology and Health
Duke University Medical Center
Durham, North Carolina

THE
FORGIVENESS
PROJECT

✝

The Startling Discovery
of How to Overcome Cancer,
Find Health, and Achieve Peace

MICHAEL S. BARRY

Kregel
Publications

The Forgiveness Project: The Startling Discovery of How to Overcome Cancer, Find Health, and Achieve Peace

Published by Kregel Publications, a division of Kregel, Inc., P.O. Box 2607, Grand Rapids, MI 49501.

The author and publisher are not engaged in rendering medical or psychological services, and this book is not intended as a guide to diagnose or treat medical or psychological problems. If medical, psychological, or other expert assistance is required by the reader, please seek the services of your own physician or certified counselor.

This book is not endorsed by or affiliated with The Forgiveness Project, a Registered Charity Number 1103922 in the United Kingdom.

All royalties from this book are donated to Assistance in Healthcare, Inc., in Philadelphia, a not-for-profit organization devoted to meeting nonmedical financial needs of cancer patients and their families.

Library of Congress Cataloging-in-Publication Data
Barry, Michael S., 1952-
    The forgiveness project : the startling discovery of how to overcome cancer, find health, and achieve peace / Michael S. Barry.
    p. cm.
1. Spiritual healing. 2. Forgiveness—Religious aspects—Christianity. 3. Cancer—Religious aspects—Christianity. 4. Cancer—Patients—Religious life. I. Title.
BT732.5.B359   2011   234'.5—dc22   2010042945

ISBN 978-0-8254-2656-8

To my beautiful children,
Sara and her husband, Jesse,
Becca and her husband, Josh;
to my delightful grandchildren,
Lilly, Molly, Jack, and Nolan;
and to my endlessly loving
and forgiving wife,
Kay.

Remember James 4:13–15.
It's only a mist.
So seek the Lord's will,
and then do it.

What we must have are those books
which come upon us like ill fortune,
and distress us deeply,
like the death of one we love better than ourselves. . . .
A book must be an ice axe to break the sea frozen inside us.
FRANZ KAFKA

CONTENTS

9

ACKNOWLEDGMENTS

RICHARD J STEPHENSON, founder and chairman of the board of Cancer Treatment Centers of America, is a visionary whose life has been dedicated to curing cancer. In those who follow his lead, he has instilled the belief that healing and hope require addressing the underlying causes of cancer, which include providing support for the patient's psychological, spiritual, and emotional well-being. I want to thank Mr. Stephenson and his leadership team, including Roger Cary, John McNeil, Kane Dawson, and most recently Kristin Mullen, for their encouragement to pursue forgiveness education research and program development at Cancer Treatment Centers of America. I also want to respectfully remember Mary Brown Stephenson, Richard Stephenson's mother, whose memory motivates and inspires our entire organization to win the fight against cancer every day.

The Reverend Luis Cortes, president of Esperanza, the largest Hispanic faith-based evangelical network in the United States, and board member at Cancer Treatment Centers of America in Philadelphia, encouraged me to write this book. Truth be known, he was the catalyst that started the ball rolling. God puts special people in our lives who subtly (and sometimes not so subtly) influence our decisions. I am very grateful that God put Luis in my life.

The book you hold in your hands can be traced back to Luis and his passion to make the good news known to all.

Josh Bishop is one of my very smart and talented sons-in-law. Besides being a wonderful father to my grandson Jack, and a loving husband to my daughter Becca, Josh has helped me enormously on this book. When it comes to writing, the rule of thumb is "write it first, and then write it right." I wrote it first. Josh wrote it right. Thank you, Josh. You are a better husband, father, and writer than I ever thought about being, and I am proud to have had the opportunity to work with you on this book.

Most importantly, I would like to thank my enemies, both real and perceived. You were not always wrong. You were not always right. But you were used by God to teach me what I will now attempt to share with others: the healing power of forgiveness. And I wish you well.

INTRODUCTION
Cancer and Hatred

Is THERE A RELATIONSHIP between the insidious disease of cancer and the sinister, life-threatening emotion of hatred? Aside from hatred's obvious cancerlike forces, which destroy families, neighborhoods, and cities and affect geopolitical relationships around the world, I have wondered about its impact at the cellular level. Do hatred and anger affect us molecularly, making us vulnerable to disease—including the Big C, cancer? This book presents a reasonable answer to the question, and it offers reasonable solutions. Further, it allows us to witness the unity of modern medicine and ancient wisdom, as well as the healing of body, mind, and spirit that results from this integration.

At Cancer Treatment Centers of America in Philadelphia, the pastoral care department conducts educational forgiveness programs for patients who self-identify strong feelings of anger, hatred, and a need to forgive others, themselves, or, on occasion, God. The forgiveness program takes a minimum of three hours: one hour in the office going over the material, a one-hour homework assignment, and after engaging with the material, another hour with the department to process the patient's experience. After four years of research, including countless forgiveness programs conducted with many of our patients, I've reached this conclusion:

> The stress of unforgiveness* negatively affects the immune system. Forgiveness, on the other hand, has an immediate, wholesome effect and long-term benefit in strengthening the immune system and positively affecting the healing process.

Because of the variables associated with ministering to a cancer patient population, we do not have the luxury of entering into a long-term therapeutic relationship with our patients. Some treatment regimens last for weeks at a time, while others require only a two-hour chemotherapy session in which the patient comes and goes from the hospital before we even know they are there. Some come only for a second opinion and choose not to receive treatment at the hospital. Others receive treatment for longer periods and either get better or enter a hospice program. Such is the nature of cancer, cancer treatment, and ministry to these wonderful people.

Because we are only absolutely certain to see patients during their three-day initial evaluation, our education program is designed to be compact, focusing on what we consider the essence of forgiveness. We plant seeds and occasionally have the opportunity to see the fruit of our labors.

This book attempts to share what we do, and how and why we do it, as well as what we have learned along the way.

The authors of *Forgiveness: Theory, Research, and Practice* remind us that when it comes to forgiveness research, "one methodological size does not fit all questions and answers."[1] Not only are

---

* For our purposes, the word *unforgiveness* is intended to mean "unable or unwilling to forgive." The term is commonly used in research journals and serves as an alternative to the more cumbersome (but technically correct) unforgi*vingness*.

there various measurement methods for gaining information about forgiveness, but it is equally true that the experience of forgiveness varies.

God's intervention into people's lives is always shrouded in mystery. Over the years, I have witnessed more than a few miraculous healings, both spiritually and physically. I hope that my firsthand experience of extraordinary phenomena—and my attribution of them to God—will not preclude the initiation of a serious conversation about the healing power of forgiveness. Most scientists, generally less comfortable with religious phenomena, would probably categorize the power of forgiveness in much the same way they categorize similar, inexplicable phenomena in the world of cancer: as *spontaneous remission* (such as what takes place when cancerous tumors suddenly disappear). However, God can change a human heart in an instant if we are willing and he desires.

Many of my colleagues in forgiveness research believe that "forgiveness is not a simple solution; the development of positive emotional, cognitive, and behavioral changes following an offense takes time and effort."[2] Although it can take time and effort, *time and effort are not the most important ingredients of forgiveness.* Sometimes, God does extraordinary things in very little time and with very little effort, if a person's heart is in the right frame: willing and ready. My forgiveness program cannot make a person's heart willing or ready, but good things often happen when one is open to the possibility of change.

The best parts of this book are the stories told by a number of my patients who have discovered peace through the healing power of forgiveness while fighting for their lives against cancer.

You will conclude, I hope, that if these people were able to face and forgive their demons, you can face and forgive yours as well. If so, you will be well on your way to an unparalleled experience that can best be described, in a good way, as *peaceful indifference.*

Aristotle offers this deeply profound thought: "The best friend is the man who, in wishing me well, wishes it for my sake."[3] Is it possible to reach an emotional plateau where we can truthfully offer well wishes to those who have hurt us, in many cases, very deeply? The stories you will read in this book suggest that it is.

The remainder of this book contains the information I share with my patients at the beginning of their search for personal wellness through forgiveness. They have found it helpful, and I hope you will as well.

Václav Havel, former president of the Czech Republic, once said:

> We have become morally ill because we have become accustomed to saying one thing and doing another. We have learned not to believe in anything, not to care about one another, and only to look after ourselves. Notions such as love, friendship, compassion, humility, and forgiveness have lost their depth dimension.[4]

A premise of this book is that *moral illness* often results in our repressing hatred and anger to the point that they breed a wide array of illnesses, both physical and social.

President Havel's solution? "Only a new spiritual vision—cosmic in its dimensions and global in scope—can rescue civilization."[5]

The new spiritual vision sought by Václav Havel is an old one. Rooted unambiguously in every ancient religion, the rescue of civilization begins and ends with forgiveness.

Rev. Dr. Michael S. Barry
Philadelphia, Pennsylvania

Chapter 1

COOLING THE FIRE WITHIN

Of the Seven Deadly Sins, anger is possibly the most fun. To lick your wounds, to smack your lips over grievances long past, to roll over your tongue the prospect of bitter confrontations still to come, to savor to the last toothsome morsel both the pain you are given and the pain you are giving back—in many ways it is a feast fit for a king. The chief drawback is that what you are wolfing down is yourself. The skeleton at the feast is you.

FREDERICK BUECHNER, *BEYOND WORDS*

An injury, such as a bruised and twisted ankle, produces inflammation (swelling) and heat, which is why we put an ice pack on it. Infection, exposure to toxins, and other types of trauma produce inflammation as well. According to the National Cancer Institute, "chronic inflammation appears to contribute to tumor [growth] of different cancers."[1] Further, "people who regularly take anti-inflammatory medication (Advil, Nurofen, ibuprofen, etc.) are less vulnerable to cancer than people who do not."[2] It would appear that, in many situations, *if you can control the inflammation, you can control the disease.*

Ice for a swollen ankle. Antibiotics for a sinus infection. But what can you put on an injured, wounded, angry heart? We suggest cooling the internal fire with forgiveness.

The best . . . *after*

Though this book is about forgiveness and not about elite competition, both have a similar goal. At the heart of competition is the desire to strive and struggle, to push back against anything that might force us to settle for second best, anything that might compromise our dreams, goals, ideals, health, or values.

The same desire lies at the heart of forgiveness.

This book is written for those who refuse to allow their lives to be destroyed by anger, hatred, or revenge—the fire within. It's for anyone who chooses to run the narrow road reserved for the elite—those who strive to be the best they can be. It applies to everyone who desires to be the best person; the best athlete; the best Christian, Hindu, Buddhist, Muslim, or Jew; the best parent or friend. It encompasses the best of what it means to be healthy and fully alive; the best of what it means to be a human being. Most important, it addresses the core needs of everyone who desires to be the best *after*.

After you've been treated unfairly.

After you've been abused or hurt.

After your good name has been slandered.

After your marriage has shipwrecked.

After your heart has been broken by meanness and betrayal.

After you have been victimized by friend or foe.

After you've been tortured or traumatized.

After your physician has stolen your hope.

If you want your joyful, happy life back, *after* these sorts of things, you must follow in the footsteps of those rare people who refuse to quit, who choose to regain the happiness their pain has taken away.

By now, most people are aware of Lance Armstrong's story: how he overcame testicular and brain cancer that had metastasized to his lungs. How did he do it? Through a combination of top medical treatment and sheer desire. Here's part of what we know about top athletes, in particular, that sets them apart: In spite of their unique strengths, champions are regular people who face the same motivational ebbs and flows we all do. "Top athletes may seem like a distinct species from the rest of us, but they also represent what's possible in each of us," says Jay Kimiecik, author of *The Intrinsic Exerciser: Discovering the Joy of Exercise.* "They set lofty goals, then push themselves, trying and testing every tool, technique, and method to stay motivated."[3]

Elite patients don't settle

Elite athletes seem to have one thing in common: the strong desire to excel. Cancer patients have their own elite class too. Medical oncologist Dr. Bernie Siegel refers to these people as *exceptional cancer patients.*[4]

Would you be surprised if I told you that the patients who are most likely to engage in the forgiveness program we offer are usually pretty exceptional people? They are otherwise normal people who, for whatever personal reason, have a certain drive, desire, and relentless ability to identify a goal and reach it. These patients explore every opportunity to find healing for their bodies. *They are willing to struggle, because there is no other way to beat the competition—or the odds.*

You can imagine the courage it takes for some people to sit before a stranger—an unknown pastor like me, for example—and seek the healing that only forgiveness can offer. It's a triumph of the human spirit to even *try* to heal a painful past! But these few brave ones—who, for their own reasons and in their own ways, are overachieving, pushing themselves beyond the norm, yearning and struggling for a peace that once eluded them—have chosen to battle years of complacency and to settle no more.

Shedding their anger and hatred, these exceptional people seek to regain balance, wholeness, and joy in their lives through forgiveness. As the Bible reminds us, and we do well to remember, "In a race all the runners run, but only one gets the prize[.] Run in such a way as to get the prize."[5]

This book is different

I can understand if you're thinking, *There are hundreds of books about forgiveness; how different could this one be? I've read other books on the topic and they didn't seem to help.* Believe me, you're not alone.

This book is different in three important ways. I'll expand on each of these later in the chapter and throughout the book, but we'll start with a brief introduction.

First, this book attempts to answer the question of whether there is a relationship between cancer and unforgiveness. Everyone knows that anger and hatred often destroy our families, marriages, and communities, but can these raw emotions have equally destructive consequences (including cancer) for our physical well-being? And, if so, can forgiveness help heal the disease? I intend to show that, yes, there is a relationship between cancer and unforgiveness.

Second, although research suggests that "emotional forgiveness can be achieved using a variety of therapeutic interventions,"[6] most books I've read on the topic of forgiveness offer advice based on a set number of steps (3, 4, 5, 10, or even 20). I don't think it works that way. My experience is that some people require more steps than others—and other people require fewer—but what it usually boils down to is one or two key insights that seem to unlock the door, enabling the person to forgive. This book is about gaining *insights* instead of taking *steps*.

Finally, this book will appeal to those who are open to explore the mysterious and unpredictable *spiritual* aspects of life, wherein the healing and peace we find is experienced as a gift from God. Our healing is a result of our willingness to regain balance in our lives—spiritually, physically, and emotionally. I intend to show that God moves within the heart that is willing to forgive.

Is this book only for the religious? No. And if you're not particularly religious, I hope that my extraordinary religious experiences don't keep you from giving serious consideration to my conclusions.

I am a serious theologian, who is just as puzzled by these experiences as anyone else. But they have helped shape my understanding of God and informed my experience of forgiveness.

Rest assured that my religious views will be expressed with sensitivity to the fact that you may not share my beliefs. I am not trying to convert anyone to my faith. But to the extent that you share my Christian beliefs, this book may helpfully inform your understanding of the gospel.

To be sure, Christianity does not have a cornerstone on forgiveness. Pain, anger, and needless suffering know no boundary and are shared by people of every age, race, and creed. People without faith in God can and do discover the ability to forgive; but it is fair to say that every religion I have examined, including my own, highly values forgiveness, suggesting that, for many, the experience of forgiveness is a journey into the very heart of God.

The mysteries of forgiveness

Mystery is one of a handful of words that, in my view, characterize the process of forgiveness.

Mystery: The journey toward forgiveness often includes an encounter with the unexpected.

Desire: Why do some people want to forgive while others don't?

Humility: Why do we often find it difficult to see our own flaws?

Truth-seeking: Only truth can set us free from our anger and hatred.

Miracle: Any time a heart hardened by hatred is transformed into a heart of flesh, it is a miracle.

Not only do these words characterize the nature of forgiveness as I understand it, but they also characterize my experience of God.

The first of my experiences with God taught me that there is more to our humanity than our physical being; we have a soul that lives on after death. I believe "if there is a natural [physical] body, there is also a spiritual body."[7]

At the age of twenty, long before I had any interest in God, I fell out of a boat while inner-tubing on a lake in Texas. The propeller hit my right arm and hand, causing obvious damage and a near fatal loss of blood. While I was being transferred to a Red Cross boat, my soul left my body and I watched, dispassionately, as several medics attempted to stop the bleeding; all of this from twenty-or-so feet above the activity in the boat.

Recently, at a fellowship luncheon after a worship service at Second Calvary Baptist Church in Hopewell, New Jersey, patrolman Eric J. of the New York City Police Department told me of his own "out-of-body experience." Now retired, Eric had been hit by a car, one fateful morning, while riding a motorcycle patrol. The impact threw him six feet into the air, shattered his left leg, and severed his femoral artery, causing him to bleed profusely.

By God's grace, the doctors were able to save Eric's leg—and his life; but while awaiting medical treatment, he had an experience similar to mine. His soul, he said, came out of his body and looked very calmly at those attending to his physical needs. He was surprised that he felt so calm. He wasn't even afraid of dying. All he had on his mind was some unfinished business—some people he had yet to forgive.

I was fascinated by this. At the edge of death, the only thing he thought of was the burden of unforgiveness in his heart.

My conversion experience didn't come until years after my boating accident. One Thursday night, at the age of twenty-nine, after suffering the misery of depression for some time, I got on my knees in my living room and gave my life to Jesus Christ. The following Sunday, I *heard* my first sermon, even though I had attended church regularly for years. After years of indifference, the Bible suddenly became the most important book in the world to me.

I know that God exists and can do extraordinary things in people's lives, including the transformation of our hearts. I know this because he transformed mine. Forgiveness is evidence of the power of God to change the human heart.

A wisp of smoke

It's one thing to know that God exists; it's another thing entirely to know his will. Another mysterious experience, years later, cemented this lesson forever in my mind.

One Monday morning, in my office at the church where I was pastor at the time, while I was discussing the events of the weekend with the church secretary, Cindy, a small ribbon of odorless smoke suddenly appeared out of nowhere.

I saw it at first out of the corner of my eye, about two feet from my face—close enough that I could see it clearly as I turned my head to look. The smoke was grayish white, about eight inches long and an inch wide, and it disappeared almost as quickly as it had materialized. Cindy saw it too, although she described the dimensions as a little bit longer.

Needless to say, we were both startled. We looked at each other, bewildered, and immediately began to look for sources of smoke—candles, matches, or any other flame in my office. There was nothing. You might think that light from the window had briefly illumined some dust particles, but my office had thick, red velvet draperies that were fully drawn. There was simply no natural explanation.

Cindy and I both knew that it was a supernatural event; God was doing something for some reason. But what? The answer eluded us until several weeks later, when my wife, Kay, found what we called "the meaning of the mist" in the Bible:

> Now listen, you who say, "Today or tomorrow we will go to this or that city, spend a year there, carry on business and make money." Why, you do not even know what will happen tomorrow. *What is your life? You are a mist that*

appears for a little while and then vanishes. Instead, you ought to say, *"If it is the Lord's will, we will live and do this or that."*[8]

Through that strange and inexplicable event, God imprinted on my heart and mind a particular truth: *Life is short, like a mist,* and the only thing we need to worry about is doing God's will. Because every religion values forgiveness, it seems we should find common ground on the truth of God's will to forgive.

Justice is important, and righting wrongs is also God's will; but without forgiveness, at what point does the violence stop? What keeps our anger from spilling over into hateful revenge, blood-feuding, and fostering cycles of violence that threaten our own well-being as well as that of countless others? Following 9/11, what if our nation had opened a national conversation about the meaning of forgiveness in light of the tragedy? I think we might have been "shocked and awed."

Instead, as a nation, including the Christian community, we took the road well traveled, with predictable results. Had we taken the high road of forgiveness, we still would have sought justice for the perpetrators, but perhaps some better decisions would have been made along the way. Here's my question: Following the attacks on the Pentagon and the World Trade Center, did we, first and foremost, seek God's will, or did a passion for revenge override a more faithful response? Did we pray for our enemies? Did we bless them or curse them?[9] What impact, if any, did God's Word have on the outcome of events?

For the record, I am not a pacifist. Evil must be confronted. But our best hope for conquering evil, according to the Bible, is "'not by might nor by power, but by my Spirit,' says the Lord Almighty."[10] In retrospect, I wish there had been, at a minimum, a national conversation on forgiveness, so that in the end we might have a more secure sense that the road we are traveling together in the War on Terror is the high road. Life is a mist. The only thing that matters is doing God's will.

Is healing really possible?

The easy answer to this question would be to quote Matthew 19:26: "With God all things are possible"—and to ask you to take it on faith. But it would be far more effective, I think, to share what I *know* rather than what I *believe*; to share the miraculous healings I've actually seen with my own eyes.

I'm a Presbyterian, and as a general rule, Presbyterians don't talk much about dramatic healings. We don't think much about healing, and for the most part don't even pray for it. In fact, we're pretty suspicious of those who do. When Presbyterians do pray for healing, we typically pray that the doctors will do their job well and that healing will be the result of their God-given abilities and medical training—a special dispensation of love and grace. We usually don't pray for someone to be healed by God in an extraordinary way.

I hadn't either—until Dean called me. I was sitting in my church office when the phone rang.

"Mike, is there any way you could come to my home and pray for me? I just got back from the doctor and got some bad news."

Dean had just learned that the numbness in his leg was caused by a tumor on his spine.

"I will gladly come and pray for you," I said.

Remembering a small vial of oil that was in my desk drawer, though I had never used it, and being cognizant of the verse in James that says we should anoint the sick with oil in the name of the Lord, I took the vial with me to Dean's house and touched a bit of oil to his forehead as I prayed and asked God to heal his body. The prayer was simple and short, and before long I was on my way back to the church.

Three hours later, as Dean later told me, he was watching TV in his recliner when his body suddenly became enveloped with waves of warmth, oscillating from his head to his feet. Back and forth, back and forth, for about ten minutes. He had faith enough to know that God was doing *something*, but he wasn't quite sure what it was.

When the warmth went away, Dean touched his legs and found that the numbness had almost completely disappeared. By the next morning, it was completely gone. Three days later, he went to have an MRI and schedule surgery to have the tumor removed, only to find that it had completely disappeared. All they could find was a speck the size of a piece of pepper.

Scientists often refer to such occurrences as *spontaneous remission*. Dean called it a miracle.

Allen, a member of my congregation in the Chicago area, also experienced spontaneous remission. Scheduled to have one-third of his stomach removed on a Wednesday morning, he had kept this information to himself until the day before the surgery. After our weekly Bible study on Tuesday, we prayed for Allen to be healed—again in accordance with James 5:14, with a simple prayer and anointing with oil.

In a recent e-mail message, here is how Allen recalls the situation:

> Examinations by colonoscopy and endoscopy, as well as X-ray, indicated a stomach ulcer. Drug therapy had no effect on the ulcer and further endoscopy and CT scan during the last six months of 2002 established the need to remove a portion (1/3) of the stomach in order to eliminate the possibility of existing or future cancer. The surgery was scheduled for December 27. Prayers were offered by Pastor Barry and an elder of Hope Church (and other persons known and unknown) before, during, and after the surgery, not only for the patient but also for family and members of the medical team.
>
> God answered our prayers in two very significant ways: 1) During surgery it was found that the ulcer had completely healed sometime after the most recent endoscopy examination; and 2) the surgery and the recovery of the patient were both very successful. Thanks be to God![11]

Wednesday morning, when the doctors operated on Allen to remove the tumor, they were surprised to find that it had completely disappeared. For unexplained reasons, it was *gone*. Today, Allen still has his entire stomach, thanks to God's divine intervention in his life.

Forgiveness – on the minds of those facing life-threatening situations

My son-in-law, Josh, tells a heart-wrenching story about his Aunt Ruthie and what was going on in her heart and mind shortly before she died of cancer:

> March 4 is the anniversary of my Aunt Ruthie's death. We had my grandma over for dinner on Monday, just so she wouldn't have to be alone all week. (I've come to think of the week before March 4 as my grandmother's annual Passion—her season of suffering.)
>
> I don't know anyone who had as much faith as Ruthie—faith that God could and would heal her. When we went to visit just days before her death (when she looked, honestly, like she was already dead), she asked us and everyone else who came into the room, "Do you believe that Jesus Christ can heal me?" If we didn't answer with an honest "Yes, absolutely," she'd ask us to leave. Of course, we all know that God chose not to heal her. And now there are two precious little boys without their mommy. It's hard to deal with, to say the least.
>
> Not long before she died, Ruthie spoke on the phone to one of her ex-husbands. I'm not sure whether *she* called him or the other way around, but at the end of the conversation, Ruthie told him, "I forgive you." Then she hung up the phone, turned to my mom, and with a look of regret on her face, said through her gaunt, parched lips, "Maybe *that* was the key"—the key to her healing.
>
> "Maybe that was the key."
>
> Four days later, she slipped into a coma; and three days after that, she died. She'd had a hard life, including four marriages—the first when she was sixteen to a man twice her age, who then abused her for the better part of two

decades. Two beautiful sons, each with a different father. Lots to forgive. But she never got around to doing that, not until she lay dying of cancer—and she suspected that being slow to forgive may have contributed to the illness that would take her life.[12]

Ruthie wasn't alone in her suspicions. This book is filled with stories of cancer patients who believe that their disease is directly tied to their unforgiveness—and, conversely, that their health is directly tied to their willingness to forgive.

More important, though, this book presents the science that tells us these people aren't crazy. As you will see, significant research has been conducted on the "biology of forgiveness," and its health benefits are now widely acknowledged.

In addition to Ruthie, the people you'll meet in the following pages—Jayne, Russie, Cathy, Rich, and Sharon—have experienced something that researchers, doctors, and scientists now understand: *cancer and unforgiveness are connected.*

Insights, not steps

Now, if we could only learn how to forgive, right? *If there really is a link between cancer and unforgiveness,* you're saying, *then just teach me how to forgive and we'll call it a day.* Sign on the dotted line, follow the yellow brick road, and set the thrusters to warp speed, Scotty.

Except it isn't that easy, is it? If life could be successfully navigated by a road map of Simple Steps to Success, we would all die old, happy, wealthy, and loved.

We all know life doesn't work that way.

I'm not going to give you a series of steps that will teach you how to forgive. Instead, I will help you uncover key insights that will lead you to forgiveness. The process of gaining *insights* instead of following *steps* is one that I like to think of as emotional or spiritual *titration.*

Titration requires extreme precision in measurement. For example, when two atoms of hydrogen bond with one atom of oxygen, suddenly an entirely new substance is created: water. The *process* of adding the precise amount of hydrogen with the precise amount of oxygen is called titration. The moment when the precise combination of hydrogen and oxygen become water is, technically, called the *equivalence point*.

Forgiveness involves a process whereby bits of information are gradually added to other bits of information. At some point, we reach an *emotional equivalence point*—an emotional release that is often described as "a feeling of lightness."

Everyone seems to have a different equivalence point. The "right mix" of information varies from person to person. In the end, we may never know which of the many insights I share will trigger the ability to forgive. There's simply no way of knowing, in advance, exactly which insights are needed; so I will share a wide array of information, hoping that you will discover what you need to know and that you will stumble across (or into) the truth that will set you free.

Some people need a teaspoon of information; others need a cup or a gallon. The only thing certain about the process of titration is the result. With forgiveness, the result is a heart mysteriously, and often unexpectedly, unburdened of anger and hatred.

Unforgiveness is spiritually cancerous to the human soul. Forgiveness, with its release of anger and hatred, is sometimes experienced spontaneously—and is nothing less than a miracle.

A posture of humility

Though God can and does miraculously heal people, both physically and spiritually, we shouldn't live our lives waiting passively for God to reach down and touch us. There are things we can do—postures of the heart that we can adopt—that will help open our lives to the mysterious work of God, like soil being softened and fertilized for a seed.

The first of these postures is *humility*.

Life has ground me down and, on more than a few occasions, worn me out. But I've been ground down in a good way, for the most part, and worn out like the Velveteen Rabbit; the kind of wear and tear that comes from helping others and attempting to alleviate suffering. Along the way, I've learned some important lessons, the kind that are usually learned the hard way.

The most humbling lesson I've learned is that my enemies and adversaries are not always wrong. Over the years, I've learned to become a better listener; I've become more open to taking seriously the thoughts and ideas and points of view of others, particularly those with whom I disagree. Wisdom has taught me that there is often no relationship between how strongly I feel about something and how right I am. In truth, I can feel very strongly about something and be completely wrong.

The second most humbling lesson is that, as formidable as my enemies and adversaries can be, I (like most people) have been my own worst enemy. My ego can be so sensitive that I have difficulty accepting that I've done anything wrong. I tend to quickly reframe the situation to put myself in the best possible light, because my ego cannot easily bear the idea that an "error in judgment" was made— much less that it caused other people pain. Like me, many people prefer to deny their guilt in harming others or themselves, choosing instead to shrug it off or pretend it didn't happen. However, an encounter with truth leaves us humbled by the fact that we have no one to blame but ourselves for the decisions we've made. A lie, on the other hand, often traps us in denial and blame.

The Potter has had his way with the clay of my life, fashioning for himself a servant that is, perhaps at long last, a vessel worth using. Before I came to faith in Jesus Christ, I was largely unaware or unconcerned about my personal behavior and its effect on other people. Over time, though, God has opened my eyes and allowed me to know myself better, enabling me to more accurately see my strengths and weaknesses.

I have been humbled in two ways by this new insight: First, I now see that *I do not fully use my strengths*; and second, *my weaknesses remain*. In sum, I am human and have learned to accept the inescapable reality that much of life is about accepting the limitations of my humanity and accepting responsibility for my behavior—which is another way of saying that I am a sinner in need of grace.

In the process of forgiveness, *first base is usually reached on our knees* in humble recognition of the basic fact that to be human means that we all make mistakes; we are all both perpetrators and victims of harm.

Driven to do it well

In addition to humility, a heart committed to forgiveness must be *driven*, committed to seeing the process through to the very end. Paul writes in 2 Timothy 4:7, "I have fought the good fight, I have finished the race, I have kept the faith." These are the words of a driven person.

I am a chronic overachiever, and have been throughout my life. God only knows why I am the way I am, but there is a long list of mostly minor accomplishments I have achieved because I am driven to work hard (and I've had some good coaching along the way).

Here are several examples: At 165 pounds, I was selected to the All-City football team in San Antonio, Texas (and later to the All-Century team at my high school). If I had played running back, this might not be noteworthy; but I played right guard, a position that, at the time, was usually filled by 200-pounders. How did I do it? Simple: I worked harder than the other guys.

When I became a parent, simply being a parent wasn't good enough. I had to take it to another level—or at least try. I became a certified parenting instructor through Active Parenting, training parents and other trainers from as far away as South Africa. When I became a Christian, it wasn't enough to sit on the sidelines, so I gave up a lucrative career and went to seminary. I later received a doctorate in ministry.

In other words, whatever I did, I wanted to do well. Very well.

My drive to succeed (or overachieve, as the case may be) has forced me out of complacency and into the occasionally exhausting world of *struggling*—struggling against "the world"; struggling to identify and overcome obstacles to goals; and struggling against, more than anything else, my own "shadow self," the part of my inner being that whispers words like "It doesn't matter." "Quit!" "No one cares." "What difference does it make?" "What difference do *you* make?"

My shadow self, or sinful self, would have me believe that trying to help people learn how to forgive is a waste of time; that if, after two thousand years, Christianity hasn't cemented the importance of forgiveness in the hearts and minds of the faithful, what makes me think my efforts will yield a worthwhile result?

The short answer is simple: I don't know that it will. Not surprisingly, though, if my Christian faith requires me to forgive, then I must be willing to at least try, and to try hard if necessary. I know it has made a difference in the lives of many of my patients and has already borne fruit in their families. Perhaps it might bear fruit in the lives of many others, as well. But it hasn't happened in the lives of my patients without effort.

What is your shadow self whispering in your ear right now? Probably the same thing my shadow self whispers in mine. But I am here to tell you this: Your life matters! God cares! Don't quit! Life is worth living; it is worth fighting for! You can release your painful past and find healing through forgiveness!

Cancer Treatment Centers of America in Philadelphia is pioneering the integration of forgiveness education more broadly into our culture through a program called *Release!* Perhaps a new norm can be established, a new emotional baseline created, that reflects a new and better appreciation for the importance of the health and well-being of a person's soul in the endless quest for personal peace and physical healing.

Forgiveness is not the norm in our society. Against the backdrop of an increasingly secular culture, any serious attempt to forgive entails walking the road less traveled. In our violent and hate-filled culture, vengeance is the norm at one extreme, and apathy at the other—both of which lead to poor health, in body, mind, and spirit, as well as in family, community, and culture. The wave of love, human decency, and forgiveness continues to ebb. If we attempt to swim against the flow, everyone else will think we're heading in the wrong direction. But we're not. We're headed toward abundant living.

Though we may experience spiritual and emotional atrophy, our strength can be regained and our lives can be revitalized. But not without effort. To underscore the importance of effort, consider this:

> People who are able to forgive have significantly less depression and are significantly less likely to committ suicide.[13]

> Forgiveness therapy is recognized as a powerful method of breaking cycles of hostility, anger, and hatred.[14]

Unforgiveness is equivalent to emotional suffocation, often resulting in the feeling that our lives are not worth living. Forgiveness should be the norm in our culture, and perhaps one day it will be; but until then, it will be embraced primarily by the driven few who desperately want to live full, healthy, and peaceful lives.

Five smooth stones

The Bible tells the story of a young shepherd named David, who was pitted in battle against a giant, Philistine warrior named Goliath. On the battlefield, Goliath was dressed in full battle regalia, including armor and a spear, while David had only his faith and a slingshot. But David was undaunted. He chose five smooth stones from a stream and put them in his shepherd's bag. Then, with slingshot in hand, he approached the giant.

The mighty warrior taunted David, saying, "Am I a dog, that you come at me with sticks?"[15]

David replied that he came in the power of God, and that God would deliver the Philistine into his hand. Then, reaching into his bag, he felled the giant with a single stone.[16]

I have selected the stories of five cancer patients to share with you. Each story of finding forgiveness is unique. For one person, the key was grappling with the idea of *fairness*. Another person was able to *spontaneously* forgive those who had harmed her. A third person experienced a *dream* in which God convinced her that she must forgive, followed by a heartfelt decision to release her hatred. The fourth person was trapped by the all-too-common inability to *empathize* with mean, sick, and sinful people. And the fifth person learned the value of *prayer* and the importance of *listening to God*.

All five faced their giants and felled them with forgiveness. In that sense, their stories represent "five smooth stones." Perhaps one of their stories will inspire and empower you to conquer whatever giants you are struggling with, helping you to face them and forgive them.

The people whose stories you're about to read all love life and have refused to let anything interfere with their health and well-being. They didn't choose their paths of suffering, but they have emerged through their difficulties with their well-deserved anger mysteriously dissolved by forgiveness.

If you need a step program, there are hundreds of other books that might help you. If you want to understand forgiveness and explore the possibility of finding it, this book may be for you.

> Small is the gate and narrow the road that leads to life, and only a few find it.[17]

The Stories

Attachment to a hurt arising
from a past event
blocks the inflow of hope
into our lives.

ST. JOHN OF THE CROSS,
A SIXTEENTH-CENTURY CARMELITE MYSTIC

Chapter 2

JAYNE
"A Feeling of Lightness"

*Everyone says that forgiveness is a lovely idea until
they have something to forgive.*
C. S. LEWIS, *MERE CHRISTIANITY*

AMONG THE MORE dramatic miracles I've witnessed is the one experienced by Jayne Rager, which is described in this chapter. No story incorporates the principles of finding forgiveness more than hers. She is the poster child for finding and living in freedom.

After she developed cancer, she learned how to battle her way back into good health, leaving no stone unturned. She sought out *every possible* advantage in her fight against cancer, including the benefits of forgiveness taught at Cancer Treatment Centers of America.

Today, she eats a healthy macrobiotic diet, exercises regularly, and even does chin-ups in her living room. (Can you do a chin-up?) Jayne has a publishing contract for a book she's writing and was featured in a *Dateline NBC* program about her tragic experience in Mexico.

Here is her story.

In June 2007, on a little-traveled country road less than a mile from their home in San Miguel de Allende, Mexico, Jayne Rager Garcia Valseca and her husband, Eduardo, were surrounded by armed men and dragged from their Jeep at gunpoint. Eduardo was struck on the head with a hammer. Injured and frightened, the couple were forced into another car, their wrists and ankles bound with duct tape and pillowcases pulled over their heads.

The day hadn't started like this, of course. Summer vacation was just around the corner, and the Valsecas and their three children were looking forward to the break. The family lived on a ranch just outside the small town where Jayne and Eduardo had founded a not-for-profit elementary school for the town's children—including their own. They dropped their kids off at school that morning, and on the short drive home their lives changed forever.

Jayne's journey—at least as it applies to the topic of this book—begins here, at the depths of despair and sadness. And I don't think it will ruin the story to tell you that her journey has brought her to the emotional heights of forgiveness, which she describes as *a feeling of lightness*.

She certainly had a lot to forgive. About twenty minutes after the abduction, she was dropped off on the side of the road with only a ransom note to keep her company. "We have your husband," it said in Spanish. Her husband was held captive for nearly eight months. He spent much of the time in a box no bigger than a small closet, with just enough room to stand up or lie down. He was kept naked on a hard, cold, rough floor, tortured with beatings and with blinding light and loud music day and night. He was shot twice at close range, once in the arm and once in the leg. Several of his ribs were broken.

For her part, Jayne spent some thirty long weeks in a living hell. "There were moments when I thought that I couldn't possibly go on," she said. The criminals sent her photographs of her husband to coerce her into paying a multimillion-dollar ransom, one that she couldn't afford to pay even if she were willing to deal with these horrible men. Eduardo's captors forced him to write notes and make phone calls at gunpoint. Throughout the whole experience, Jayne "felt the deepest kind of hatred for these people and what they were doing to me and my family."

Jayne says this of her thoughts of revenge: "These thoughts became fantasies of all of the creative ways I could torture them, even kill them. My favorite one was of being a giant, female Samurai, beheading all of them in one clean sweep of my sword. Thinking about these things brought me great pleasure."

Not necessarily the best thoughts for a person to have, but certainly understandable for a woman in Jayne's horrific predicament.

Although she felt helpless against these feelings and emotions, Jayne knew they would do her absolutely no good on the inside—especially since she had already battled cancer. Jane had been diagnosed with inflammatory breast cancer in 2005. After going through conventional treatment (along with several holistic therapies), she found herself cancer-free, full of energy, and happy to be alive.

The emotional trauma brought on by the kidnapping threatened to change all that. "I knew the negative potential it could have," she said. "I sought professional help, which was hugely comforting, but my anger, rage, and resentment were extremely hard to get a handle on."

Jayne wasn't terribly surprised when her breast cancer returned in the spring of 2008. She wasn't surprised, but she *was* devastated. She was almost numb.

What else could be taken from me? she asked. *Why me? How could all of this be happening to me?*

Still, it made sense when she thought about all of the unresolved rage she had been clinging to for so many months. Jayne realized that in order to heal completely—physically, emotionally, and spiritually—she needed to go in a different direction than before. Her search for a holistic approach to cancer care led her to Cancer Treatment Centers of America's Eastern Regional Medical Center in Philadelphia, and then to my office for a conversation about forgiveness.

The first time I met Jayne, she was wearing her trademark straw cowboy hat, the kind that rolls up easily on the side and can be shaped in a pointed fashion to easily cover her eyes. She wore a pink bandana underneath to mitigate the all-too-common embarrassment of losing her hair. Though she is Caucasian, her time in Mexico lent a Hispanic flair to her clothing. Almost always, she was able to maintain her natural beauty and usually displayed the all-important cheerful, hopeful, and optimistic attitude that is, as the experts tell us, the telltale sign of long-term cancer survivors. As hopeful as she was, though, she was always rightfully concerned about her health and her future. Jayne wanted to live.

By this time, Eduardo had been released from his captors. At the end of January, two months before Jayne's second diagnosis, she had recovered her husband—though when he returned, he was almost unrecognizable. His weight had dropped from 160 pounds to ninety.

Despite his injuries and depleted physical condition, Eduardo came back ready to jump into life, grateful for every breath of freedom. He was amazed that he could go to the refrigerator and eat whatever he wanted, that he could talk with others whenever he wanted—or at all. He was immensely thankful for everything that you and I take for granted. Strangely enough, he didn't seem to have forgiveness issues with his captors. He wasn't angry. His happiness at being alive, free, and home with his family overrode any hatred, anger, or bitterness.

Jayne, on the other hand, was still stuck in her desire for revenge. She was angry and hated the kidnappers for what they had done to her family. She hated them with all her heart. Jayne had become so hardened that she hadn't been able to cry for months. At times, she would shake uncontrollably, but she could no longer shed even one tear. She had been running on adrenaline, like a soldier on the front lines of battle, afraid that if she let her guard down all would be lost. Her way of processing things (or *not* processing them) was her way of surviving, and it worked—but it took a toll, and now she had breast cancer again.

As I talked with Jayne during our first meeting, it became apparent that she was aware of her need to forgive, her need to let go of all the negative emotion that she kept bottled up inside. But, like so many people, she hadn't figured out exactly how. She needed more direction in order to apply it to her life in a new, permanent way—one that she hoped would help her along the road to health and wholeness.

In short, she needed to let go of her painful memories. She needed a clean slate.

I'll let Jayne tell the next part of the story:

> At one of our first meetings, we talked for about an hour. Dr. Barry heard my story and was compassionate, but to my surprise I didn't get a whole lot of sympathy. Now, don't get me wrong: he was sympathetic, but that was not his focus. I had kind of gotten used to having people cry when I told them the story; they would embrace me and mirror my feelings of injustice. Dr. Barry's reaction was very different. It was nonjudgmental. The conversation was more about his wanting me to find peace again, which often requires learning to feel empathy toward the kidnappers. At one point, he even suggested that there might be some self-righteousness in what I was feeling. Well, that was the *last* thing I wanted to hear. I wanted to hear about how right I was to feel the way I felt, how wrong and despicable they were, and that sooner or later there would be some sort of divine justice.[1]

Jayne wasn't having it. She told me how she had already tried to find empathy for the men who had taken so much from her. She had even tried praying for them. She had tried to find forgiveness in the midst of her pain and had come up empty-handed.

"How in the world can I find empathy for these reptiles?" she asked me. "They ambush you, snatch you from your life and your family. We lost our home, our business. We were devastated financially. We had to flee the country leaving our belongings behind, everything we had worked for for seventeen years and built as law-abiding citizens. I lost my health from the months of stress, and my children are traumatized. How can I *possibly* find empathy for these horrible individuals who kidnap, destroy families, and harm and kill people for money?"

I never suggested that life was fair or that forgiveness would be easy.

I reminded Jayne that, under the right circumstances, every one of us is capable of great evil. No one is exempt—not Jayne, not you, and not me. This isn't easy to hear, of course, but it's true.

"It's not about them, Jayne," I said. "They've moved on, maybe to the next victim. You're still angry and they probably haven't given you a second thought. You are only harming yourself by holding on to this. Forgiveness is a gift that you can give to yourself. As a concept, forgiveness transcends any particular religion. It's not that it's the Christian thing to do or the Jewish thing to do or the Buddhist, Muslim, or Catholic thing to do. It's the right thing to do, if what you want is the best chance of beating your disease. It's the human thing to do.

"This is what you can do for *you*, Jayne."

I left Jayne with a homework assignment. I told her to go home and write a letter to the men who had kidnapped her husband and thrust her life into chaos. She didn't have to forgive them right then and there, and she didn't have to conjure up eloquent words for some grand pronouncement of empathy and understanding. She simply had to tell them how she felt.

Jayne's letter was five pages long. "It felt good to write it," she said. "It really did. It felt like some kind of emotional release. Like getting it off my chest."

The next time I met with Jayne, we talked about the letter and about how she felt while writing it.

"It felt good," she told me, "but I'd feel even better if I had an address to send it to, and maybe just a tiny bit of anthrax."

Funny—and honest—but not exactly what we were working

toward. I told Jayne that she should do some more writing. This time, she needed to work a little harder toward finding empathy. It isn't something that comes from the head, I told her, but from the heart.

When she sat down to write for the second time, Jayne found herself stuck, not sure what she could say that hadn't already been said. The cursor on the computer screen blinked at her silently. She decided to clear her mind and meditate on empathy. The answer eventually came to her, and when it did, it took a surprising and inspired form.

"I decided to use my creativity to create a mental movie set. I imagined the kidnappers as babies. I'm a mother of three and I adore children. I've often thought that all babies come into the world as blank canvasses. I've seen as a mother how they absorb, like little sponges, information about the world around them, about their environment. I saw these little babies in my mind, innocent and new, and then took them forward in the imaginary movie, creating what they must have gone through in order to ultimately become what they became, capable of doing what they do. I did this for each one of them, one by one. All seven of them."

Suddenly—after an hour and a half of stretching her mind and creating a script by which she could understand these men and their motives—she felt it. "I felt an enormous wave of relief," she said, "as if the weight of the world had just been lifted from my shoulders. It was amazing. I felt so much lighter."

Sharon Whitmore, a fellow cancer patient, described the result of forgiveness in similar terms. "I woke up the next day and had this feeling," she said. "It was a lightness. It was a lightness in my heart. You know how you have a heavy load? It didn't feel heavy anymore."

Moreover, and much to Jayne's surprise, she felt the most relief in the places where she had the disease. "I had gotten it off my chest"—she smiled—"literally."

The process of releasing her anger made her ask some questions, as well. *How much of this is the result of my own emotions? How much is the result of my own way of thinking and processing things?*

Jayne felt amazing for the rest of the day. She had a smile on her face that could not be contained, and a lightness in her step that was noticeable to everyone around her. She had more energy. Her chemotherapy infusions felt easier to take. Most importantly, she had a renewed love of life and was ready to move into healing.

The lesson has stayed with her and has begun to change the way she lives her life in subtle and not-so-subtle ways.

"Now, I remind myself daily to apply forgiveness to my everyday life—while driving, while in the grocery store, and at home with my family. Every time I feel myself going into anger or judgment, I instead choose empathy and forgiveness. I get better at it every day. Doing this has been life changing for me and has had a ripple effect in countless encounters."

I believe that everyone can experience the same life-changing feeling of lightness that Jayne describes. It isn't going to look the same for everybody—which is perhaps one of the reasons that forgiveness has been overlooked and underused in the recovery process. It can't be precisely quantified. The notion that the process of forgiveness requires a predetermined number of steps in order to arrive at the final destination is a notion that must be put to rest.

In short, there is no easy equation that says

$$\frac{(\text{action } a + \text{understanding } b) \text{ } \mathbf{x} \text{ } (y^2 \text{ empathy})}{x \text{ days}} = \text{forgiveness}$$

Such equations simply do not exist. There are too many psycho-spiritual variables involved for a step-by-step process to work. This isn't as easy as setting the clock on the DVD player; it's more complicated than ensuring that, at the end of the cycle, your whites are whiter and your colors brighter.

In light of how complex we are as human beings, why would we expect our emotional experiences to be identical?

This does not mean, however, that there aren't any common threads between individual stories. Even as religious conversion experiences are often quite unique, they also share similarities. So, too, is it with experiences of forgiveness.

For example, one woman tearfully approached me after a sermon I preached on forgiveness. She told me that when she learned I was preaching on forgiveness, she almost decided to skip church altogether. Instead, she decided to stay. During the sermon, "something happened." What happened can be explained spiritually as a miracle, for anytime a heart hardened by hatred is transformed, suddenly or otherwise, into a heart of flesh able to forgive, it is a miracle.

On the other hand, I have worked for several months with people who were unable to get to first base. In one case, after months of work, a woman harbored just as much hatred against her father as when she had begun.

Just as no two stories are the same, no two paths to forgiveness are identical.

Your path to forgiveness may happen miraculously, a change of heart at a moment's notice. Like Jayne, it may require a fresh and creative approach to discovering empathy. It may take days, weeks, months, or years. There is no way of knowing until you begin the process.

But I do know this: the most important variables are *not* the time and effort a person is willing to put toward forgiveness. Rather, it is *motivation*. It relies on whether or not a person has the wholehearted desire to let their painful past go. Without the firm desire to be healed and whole, a person could go through a hundred steps and spend many long months working at the issues at hand without ever experiencing the change of heart required for true forgiveness.

Forgiveness, then, is a process with a definable beginning and end; but the road linking them is often as distinctive as each individual.

The one trait that each story—including Jayne's—seems to share is the *strong desire to live*. Like Jayne, you must be willing to do whatever it takes to increase your quality of life, even if it means facing your demons—and forgiving them. Jayne faced her demons with anything but a feeling of helplessness. Rather, she exuded resiliency, the ability to bounce back from her situation with a strength and personal power that came from a potent will to live.

Her life, as dark as it had become, now blossoms with numerous opportunities to speak before impressive audiences. It would be trite to suggest that there is a silver lining in every cloud; but if ever there was a dream that I hoped would come true, it is the dream that is coming true for Jayne, her husband, and their wonderful children.

We'll close this chapter with some final thoughts from Jayne:

> My gratitude to Dr. Barry and everyone at Cancer Treatment Centers of America is beyond words. I believe that going through the forgiveness process has been an essential part of my recovery, and I feel so blessed to have had access to this complete approach to healing from cancer from the inside out.

Chapter 3

RUSSIE

"A Little Ugliness in the Deep Recesses of My Heart"

TODAY, RUSSIE IS A well-spoken woman who clearly enunciates her words in sentences that pour out of her with noticeable enthusiasm and infectious laughter. Her speech is so crisp and clear, it's as if she's always lived like this—but she hasn't. She lost part of her tongue to oral cancer several years ago.

When Russie first came to Cancer Treatment Centers of America, she missed the new patient orientation program we offer to our patients who have an interest in the role that pastoral care plays at CTCA. Still, I had a chance to meet with her one-on-one, and then met with her many times in the following months.

Before her surgery, she asked me to pray with her—which of course I was happy to do. The surgery was a success, at least according to the standards by which such surgeries are measured in the medical field: The cancer had been removed. The big picture, of course, was that losing a sizable piece of her tongue was a small price to pay in exchange for her health. The small picture . . . was sad and kind of tragic. I prayed with Russie following her surgery as well, and this time placed a small drop of oil on her tongue, as an anointing.

What happened next defies reason, so it might be best to let Russie tell this part of the story herself:

> After my surgery, I had real difficulty with my speech. I met with a speech therapist, and I think that was really the point at which I got a little depressed. It wasn't that I lost so much of my tongue; it was that I really wasn't going to have a chance to communicate. That worried me, because I like to talk and socialize.
>
> Mike came over and he was able to understand what I was worried about. He just said, "Do you believe in healing?" When I said, "Yes, I do," he said, "Well, I feel led to anoint you with oil and pray with you." It was a really simple prayer, just like the one before I went into my surgery.
>
> After we had our prayer, I cried because it was just so emotional. My mom went down to eat dinner, and I went to sleep for a little while. I woke up when my cell phone began ringing. I hadn't been answering it, because my husband, my family, *nobody could understand what I was trying to say*. The phone continued to ring and ring and I just thought, *I'll answer it and they'll know it's me, and that I can't talk, and they'll hang up like they always do and call back later when my mom can answer*.
>
> It was my cousin, and she was confused when she heard me. She said, "I thought you already had your surgery and you couldn't talk."
>
> I asked, "Can you understand me?"
>
> She said, "Yeah, I understand you fine; you sound just like you always do."
>
> It blew my mind, because healing was something I believed in, but I guess I thought it only happened to really good, worthy people.

But this isn't primarily a story about how Russie's speech was healed. Rather, it's a story about the healing that can happen within a person's heart. And the *very* good news is that healing (inside or out) doesn't happen only to people who are good enough or worthy enough.

"Believe me," Russie said, "in that hospital there were people who were more worthy than I was; people who were true saints, but who didn't receive that kind of healing."

Raised in a rural West Virginia coal-mining town, Russie had what she describes as a typical country childhood, complete with time spent splashing in the creek. Her family was very religious.

"I don't mean religious in a bad context," she clarified. "They're very disciplined, people of great faith. I grew up being so intimidated by that, because I was always—I wouldn't say I was the black sheep, but I was always the one who questioned everything in my heart, whether I said it to anybody or not." Russie describes herself as something of a doubting Thomas, the sort of person who had to have everything proved to her. In college, she turned away from her upbringing and went off and did her own thing.

"But when I got sick, it brought everything into sharp relief, all my shortcomings. You start to think that perhaps you might not have time to become that better person you always meant to be."

Until her disease, Russie thought the same way that many of us think. We know (or we hope) we are improving, we want to become better people, and we want to mature. But when she was diagnosed with cancer, Russie realized, "Wow this might be it. Whatever I've accomplished up to now might be it."

It's a sobering realization, isn't it? Whatever I've accomplished up to now might be it.

When Russie came in for one of her checkups, I mentioned the forgiveness program we offered. Russie didn't have severe trauma in her past—at least nothing to compare to Jayne or to so many others whose experiences of evil forever changed their lives. "My family is really easygoing," she told me. "We're not ones to hold grudges or get mad about things; we just typically don't do that."

But, as with most people, Russie had unforgiveness hiding just beneath the surface. Her struggle for forgiveness may not be as dramatic as Jayne's story, but it is no less important, and its resolution is no less life changing.

As it turned out, Russie had had a bad experience with one of her bosses, a workplace situation that had escalated quickly and turned very ugly. Even worse, though, was her unforgiveness toward an uncle who had cheated and hurt her father years before. "It's so funny," Russie said without a hint of humor. "You can get madder about something done to someone you really care about than about something done to you.

"Certainly, I was much more upset at this uncle for what he did to my father," she said. "I just never forgot it. He wasn't a very admirable guy, so it made it easier not to like him—and actually to kind of hate him, in my heart. It seemed okay, because it was justified. You tell yourself, '*That guy was really bad.*'"

Russie thought that hating her uncle was all right as long as she owned up to her feelings instead of trying to hide them. She was respectful toward him and always treated him well, but on some level she knew there was still something wrong about her attitude, something she called "*a little ugliness in the deep recesses of my heart.*"

So she agreed to work through the forgiveness program at CTCA. Russie remembers entire segments of the program, particularly the part where I shared with her that forgiveness is at the heart of the Christian faith and that we forgive others because we've been forgiven. Among other things, I encouraged her to look at her experiences as a detached observer, acknowledge what happened, and move on.

Because Russie wasn't receiving regular treatments from CTCA, I gave her a workbook and asked her to work through it on her own. To my surprise, she e-mailed me after completing only two of the six lessons.

"I was really through it by then," Russie said. She was afraid I would think she was a slacker, but she had actually arrived at the heart of her unforgiveness.

"It was very freeing," she said, "because I had this idea that if we forgive someone then we have to socialize with them; we have to be with them all the time; and we have to say, 'What you did was okay.' But we don't have to say it's okay, and we don't always have to be with them. I don't think God expects us to constantly have a pebble in our shoe."

If there was any single realization, any one epiphany, that broke through to Russie, it can be found here, in an e-mail she sent me after completing the forgiveness program:

> For the first time, I was able to see the concept you gave to us in class: If our own sins were bricks, it would look like the Great Wall of China! And it is only because of God's mercy that we are forgiven of those many sins. I realized that all the things I had done in my life did not deserve forgiveness either, but God chose to forgive me. I knew all of that intellectually, but for the first time in my life, I was able to really feel it. I think getting to that place allowed the real healing to begin.

If our own sins were bricks, the pile would look like the Great Wall of China.

Realizing this, of course, doesn't erase the pain caused by those who have hurt us, and it certainly doesn't justify the harm that was done to us. But it does help us understand that we have caused pain to others, just as we ourselves have been hurt. Something powerful happens when we come to grips with our own humanity against a backdrop of grace.

"It was the same thing as my healing," Russie said. "I wasn't healed because I was good enough; it was because I accepted it, I gave it to God. So I thought, *I have to give this part up too. I can't hold on to this, any part of it, anything that's going to slow my healing or hold me up.* It would also make me unworthy of this gift I've been given.

"I'm human. I'm still fallible. I'm nowhere near where I wish I was. Every day, you'll meet with little struggles that you have with people, but I don't hold on to any of that. I let it go."

And what of her relationships with those people who had hurt her so badly? Her boss and her uncle?

"I really thought that my forgiveness of these people would involve forgiveness *without association with them*," she said. "I just wasn't sure I could be with either one and continue to love and forgive them as I wanted to."

She was wrong.

"The boss that I had problems with has called me and sent me a Christmas card," she explained. "He had really serious heart surgery after that, and I called to see how he was. So, I kind of made the first move; but whenever I talked to him, I didn't feel the same anger. It was good that I didn't feel like I had to suppress anything or hold it down. It just wasn't there.

"And I've actually been able to do something I didn't think I could do, which is to spend time with my uncle. But I did! This summer my husband and I went and visited, and we were able to put everything that happened aside and just enjoy the visit for what it was."

No one knows better than Russie how much the process of forgiveness affected her healing.

"I think it is essential," she said. "I know a lot of people with anger issues that are just mad at everybody. They're always mad. I was never that kind of person, but I think it was significant that, with these two people in my life, I was still carrying it around. The fact that it still bothered me at all—normally I let that kind of stuff go, I don't really walk around being upset with people—I think was significant. And I needed to address it in order to feel as if I could move ahead. Not only was it essential for my healing, but also essential for me as a person. I would've hated to miss that.

"I tell people anytime they ask me about my cancer. I don't think I've ever failed to go into the story of the forgiveness project and what it meant to me.

"Nobody wants cancer," Russie added, "but there are a lot of people I know who have said, 'I'm better for having it.' So I lost some things. I don't look the same. But I think I have a cheer in my heart that wasn't there before."

As of this writing, I am happy to report that Russie remains cancer-free . . . in body, mind, and spirit.

Chapter 4

CATHY

"My Mom, My Hero"

CATHY PARKER-AAVANG's life has been more painful than she wanted it to be. Even before she was diagnosed with kidney cancer, and before it metastasized to her back, and before it formed a large tumor in the middle of her spinal cord, and before doctors told her she had two months left to live—even before all of this, Cathy's life was hard.

In some regards, her story is all too familiar.

"I had been in a twenty-five-year marriage to an alcoholic husband," Cathy explained, "and I continued to stay mostly for our four kids."

She didn't think the children could handle it if she didn't stay put and try to maintain the relationship, to keep her marriage going, despite how messy it had become.

"I didn't want them to hurt," she said. So she tried to keep it hidden from their kids. She tried to mask how destructive her husband's behavior had become. She tried to cushion the damage that was being done to all of the relationships within their family.

Resentment, anger, and unforgiveness began to fester inside.

And though Cathy eventually left her husband, she found it much more difficult to leave her emotions with him.

"In my heart, I was very unforgiving to my ex-husband for what he had put me through," Cathy said. "I had a lot of trouble forgiving him for not being there for the kids and me like I thought he should've been."

Eventually, Cathy was diagnosed with cancer. It was a huge shock, she explained, because she thought of herself as the type of person—the type of nurse, mother, grandmother, and wife—who was always in control. And now a deadly disease assaulted her, reminding her that, as much as she might think otherwise, she isn't entirely in control. No one is.

"I just couldn't believe this was happening to me—and to my family, most importantly." Her children were afraid she would die. Her new husband was understandably afraid as well. For her part, Cathy wasn't particularly afraid to die; it was more that she was afraid of leaving behind the family she had poured her whole life into.

On the upside, however, her circumstances taught her how to talk to God. More important, she learned how to *listen*. During her prayers, she began to feel a sense of oneness with God, the sort of conversations and connections that people describe with phrases like "one-on-one" or "heart-to-heart." For the first time in her life, she said, she heard God speak to her.

From these conversations with God—and from her conversations with me and others on staff at Cancer Treatment Centers of America—Cathy learned "how vitally important forgiveness is to healing."

"I felt as if God spoke *directly to me* about forgiveness," she said, "though I wasn't sure *what or whom* I had to forgive. Sometimes it's not so black-and-white in the forgiveness game, I found out."

It didn't take long for Cathy to learn that the "what" and the "whom" that she had to forgive extended far beyond her previous marriage. Cathy's *whats* and *whoms* included bad neighbors, some deep-seated things in her family, an argument or two with her husband, and what Cathy calls "the cycle of things"—those situations when more than one person or circumstance contributes to an event.

She'd also had an abusive boyfriend when she was younger. "I had never forgiven him," she said. "I just put on the hard face of 'I lived through that' and didn't give it another thought—except I hated him for what he had done to me.

"There were people I said I had forgiven but I never really had. I've learned that there's a whole different feeling when you *know* you have forgiven someone."

Cathy and I talked quite a bit about the relationship between forgiveness and healing, about the spiritual and emotional aspect of battling cancer in addition to the physical, medical aspect.

As with most of my patients who struggle with unforgiveness, I asked Cathy to write a letter to her ex-husband. In the letter, she detailed the struggles she faced during her journey toward forgiveness and wholeness.

She eventually came to the point where she could *truly* and *honestly* forgive her ex-husband. "It wasn't overnight and it wasn't easy," she said. "But I can thankfully say that I do forgive my ex-husband.

"If anything, we learned a lot from it, and we're both in a better place in our lives. We're friends now. He comes to all of our family get-togethers and picnics and is still very much a part of our kids' lives. He, too, is in another relationship and it's lovely. It's heartwarming to see that we can all be together and not have the animosity that you could feel before."

Cathy didn't know the profound impact that forgiveness would have on her healing process. She still struggles with cancer, and she's confined to an electric wheelchair as a result of nerve damage caused by the tumor in her spine. But now, nearly six years after doctors gave her only two months to live, every day feels like a victory. And her physical progress was accompanied by something that is, in many ways, more miraculous and unexpected: *it brought healing to her family.*

It started when Cathy shared with her children a letter she had written about her experience of forgiveness. "It wasn't a good-bye letter or an 'I think I'm going to die' letter—it was what I wanted them to know so they wouldn't have to struggle with the issue of forgiveness or forgiving."

The impact it had on her family was remarkable. "My kids were so touched by this letter," she told me. "I will say that, since the letter and the healing they've seen me go through—not only physically, but more important, spiritually—they are *completely different people*."

Cathy told me a heartwarming story about the change she saw within her family. It's a story I think is worth relating in her own words:

> When my youngest son, who is in college now, was a senior last year, he wrote a paper for one of his classes and it was called "My Mom, My Hero." I couldn't read it out loud because I would definitely cry, but in that paper he told the class and the teacher how one of the biggest things I had taught him was how to forgive other people and to mean it. To truly forgive someone.
>
> We went down this forgiveness trail together. Now my kids will call and say, "I know I'm supposed to forgive, but I'm really struggling," and we'll talk about it.
>
> None of us is going to be perfect at it; I'm not either. But it changed our spiritual life. *And to go from two months to live to five-and-a-half years alive?* It didn't happen because I found a different set of doctors. It happened because I found out that forgiveness is *key* in healing.

Cathy's testimony has become her family's testimony, and it's a message that should be told in classrooms (and in books) around the world. In short: *forgive.*

"Is it that easy?" Cathy asks. "No. You've got to spend time in prayer and time searching your soul to find that spot where you can say to yourself and to God, I do forgive."

Cathy's testimony includes encouragement for those without cancer as well: "Forgiveness in the whole realm of healing physically is vitally important. If you can learn it before you have to go through something like cancer—or *any* disease, or a death—then it would certainly create a life-changing experience."

"That's why I still love coming to Cancer Treatment Centers of America," she told me while at my office. "I'm doing better, but I still love coming back here and getting my checkups because of how everyone feels around here: You can't be given a pill or an IV or anything just by itself. It's got to be the whole package, and forgiveness is part of the package that goes along with healing a disease."

Chapter 5

RICH
It's Not Fair!

RICH MILTNER DIDN'T know it at the time, but his journey with cancer began with a head-on collision.

The automobile accident left him injured, and while he was seeing a doctor during his recovery, Rich was told to get his PSA levels checked. (Prostate-specific antigen is a protein that serves as a common indicator of prostate cancer.)

"I kept arguing with the guy, saying 'I'm fine, there's nothing wrong with me,' because I had no symptoms of anything," Rich said. "But the doctor was insistent that I do it."

They called him back the next morning and told him to see a doctor right away. His PSA levels were highly elevated and he needed to see a urologist immediately. After a biopsy, the urologist told Rich that he had an aggressive form of prostate cancer and he needed to seek help immediately, before it spread.

"I had no symptoms and no inclination that anything was wrong, but I was in that accident, thankfully. I mean, I was hurt, but it was a good thing and it probably saved my life."

Rich's search for treatment eventually brought him to my office at Cancer Treatment Centers of America in Philadelphia. During our new patient orientation, I met Rich and his wife and spoke with them about the various educational programs offered by the pastoral care department, including one on forgiveness. I asked him if there was anyone he was especially mad at. "No, not really," he said.

His wife disagreed. "He's got a real problem with his cousin."

I told Rich that I thought he might want to spend more time talking to me about this. When we met again later, he began telling me long, horrible stories about his experiences with one of his cousins.

Rich worked with his two cousins in a family-owned construction business they had inherited from their grandfather. It was a highly successful company that developed large commercial projects in the Cleveland area, and it was run by a very close family—at least at first.

"We all started out very young in this construction company," Rich said. "We kind of grew up in the business together, and as time went on, my cousins and I basically ran the company." Though he eventually had problems with both cousins, his relationship with the younger one became especially strained.

"I don't know what happened over the years. My younger cousin and I were really good friends—he would come over to my house, he would play Santa Claus for my kids, we did things together. But somewhere along the line as we got a little older, in our early twenties, he just turned into a different person. Our friendship ended, all the things we did socially together away from work stopped, and he turned into this controlling, angry person."

Over the next thirty-four years, Rich's working relationship with his cousin devolved into something that can only be called abusive. When describing his cousin, Rich repeatedly uses words like *creepball*, *bully*, and *backstabbing*.

"He spent the majority of his time trying to make people unhappy," Rich said. "He was full of hatred for everybody; he just got angrier and angrier." In a moment of honest clarity, Rich's cousin told him that he believed the way to get the most out of people was to belittle them. Eventually, the conflict became unbearable and Rich quit, giving two weeks' notice in the middle of a huge project for an international oil company.

We talked about why Rich had stayed in such an abusive job, and he eventually admitted that he sold out for the money. "He paid me well to abuse me, and I put up with a lot," he said.

But Rich kept telling me he had forgiven his cousin. "Listen," Rich said, "I worked for this creep for thirty-four years. I had to forgive him every day. Every day I'd walk into the shop; of course I forgave him, otherwise I wouldn't be there. I let it go, year after year. I let all this stuff go. I forgave him every day."

Though I believe Rich tried his best to forgive his cousin—or at least carry on despite his unforgiveness—other aspects of what he told me indicated that he was still carrying around the wounds that his cousin had inflicted on him. He hadn't really let any of it go.

"I had to admit that I thought about my cousin pretty much 24/7," Rich said. "I was so angry that I was obsessed. How can he be this way? How could he hurt me this way? Why would he treat me like this after all these years of faithful service?"

Rich thought of his cousin everywhere he went. "I would drive around and think, *How could you do this to me?* I would see a truck drive by with a load of concrete forms, and I'd think, *That jerk.* Even after I walked away from the business, I was still constantly thinking about all the things he said and did to me over the years."

Clearly, Rich was struggling with unforgiveness. "I was never free," he said. "His nastiness was still ruining my life."

The litany of how Rich's unforgiveness was affecting his life was exhaustive:

"I thought, you know what? That has not been healthy for my marriage," Rich said. "I was really wrong to burden my wife with all the nonsense that went on at work when I should've just left it at work, because I chose to be there. I realized at that point how it affected my marriage and my attitude toward my wife and my attitude in general. I was miserable all the time and unhappy and laying it all on her.

"And then I started thinking about my kids. What kind of father have I been to bring this home and complain about this guy and talk about him? What would my kid's lives have been like if I had not been constantly complaining?"

The negative effects of unforgiveness weren't limited to Rich's nearest and dearest either. It had unhealthy effects on Rich himself.

"At one point during all that talking about it, I realized the negative effect it was having on me, on my thought processes. It was just a matter of understanding that I was hurting *myself* at this point. It wasn't even *him* anymore; it was me being detrimental to my own well-being. I mean, my blood pressure was high, and I had other things going on besides the cancer. I wondered how much that was really affecting my health."

Over the course of our many meetings, I explained to Rich how unforgiveness can contribute to cancer—the very same material I've written about in this book.

You've heard of personality types, right? Type A, Type B, and all that? Well, I shared with Rich that research had disclosed a third type—a Type C personality. The C, of course, stands for cancer. The hallmarks of the Type C personality are kindness and chronic niceness. There's nothing that a chronically nice person wants to avoid more than conflict, because of how upsetting it can be. So, instead of confronting the abusive person, and risking the experience of a personal emotional tsunami, he or she learns to tolerate the conflict, even though its effect is like kryptonite. Toxic people can leave their corrosive residue on others, often with little or no obvious impact to their own well-being.

I explained to Rich how he was being eaten up with habitual hatred for his cousin, and how he was less likely to get physically better if he didn't get his emotional house in order, get his hatred under control. He said it made sense.

The one thing that didn't make sense, though, was why Rich had to go through the effort to forgive, if his cousin was the one who caused the problems. He kept getting hung up on the idea of *fairness*.

"I don't get what all this is about," Rick said. "I don't get the point. I'm not the one doing all these mean things. I'm not the one who's hurting other people in my life. I'm not the one causing all this stress in my life—it's this other guy. Why do I have to keep coming back here and discussing all this?

"You don't understand—I was the good guy. I put up with this. I mean, I'm a good Christian man."

In other words: *It didn't seem fair that while Rich was in such pain, there seemed to be no consequence to his cousin.* No justice. *Fairness* suggests that his cousin should be suffering for the pain he continually inflicted; but his cousin couldn't have cared less about Rich or many of the other people in his life.

Knowing that we both shared the same religious tradition, I sensed that Rich had gotten trapped in a common myth, misperception, or lie that was contributing to his inability or unwillingness to forgive. I shared a truth with Rich that I hoped might help set him free: "Rich, life isn't fair. Nowhere in the Bible is there a single verse that teaches us that life is fair. Not in this life, at least."

We spoke for a little while about "the world as it is, and not as we would have it," and I challenged him to continue the forgiveness program by writing a series of letters to his cousin, within a short period of time. I explained that his cousin would never see the letters, and he never had to tell him what was in them, but I wanted him to write what was on his heart and mind, to get it off his chest.

Rich's breakthrough, his moment of truth, his "feeling of lightness," came while writing one of those many letters. Here's how Rich describes the discovery of the truth that set him free:

> I was writing to my cousin about all the nasty, rotten things he had done to me when I started thinking about what I had been like over those last thirty years. I started to realize that I had not been the perfect Christian man I was portraying myself to be and that I truly was a sinner too.

As I sat there, I thought, *I need to ask forgiveness for all the things I've done and the way I've acted—the things I've said, the gossip.* I was more than willing to talk about *him* to anybody who was willing to listen. So I sat there and I asked forgiveness for that.

And it wasn't just the gossip. "There were times when I blew up at him and I screamed and yelled at him," Rich confessed. "I lost it and I screamed at him. I mean, I was never vulgar, I just told him off. So I started thinking, 'I'm not this perfect guy.'"

That night was a real turning point for me. After weeks of arguing that I wasn't the bad guy, it dawned on me that I'm a sinner like everybody else, and I need forgiveness.

I knew right then and there that I *had* to forgive him. I had no choice; I had to do it. I have to look at my cousin and say, 'You know what? He's not a good guy. He's not a nice man. But I need to let this stuff go. I gotta forgive him.'"

I met with Rich the following day, and he told me about his experience. It hadn't even been twenty-four hours, and already he felt different.

"I felt free," he explained. "I felt released. I felt this great weight being lifted off of me. I felt like I could truly forgive this person—and I did forgive him. I can love him now like God loves me. I can forgive him the way God has forgiven me."

Unlike for Russie and Cathy, the path of forgiveness for Rich was not the path of reconciliation. To be honest, he was fairly worried about this, worried that forgiving his cousin meant that he had to go to him and tell him, "I forgive you," or be in a relationship with him again. But that's not what forgiveness means. Some people—people like Rich's cousin—are toxic, and victims should no more be around toxic people than they should be around poison or any other harmful substance.

"When I realized that I could let it go and I don't have to have a relationship with him, I felt freed by that," Rich said.

"Things got to the point that when I would see a concrete truck full of forms go down the street and think about all the crazy stuff he made me do, I could just pray for him. I could say, 'Lord, it's coming back and he did do those things, but I don't want it to affect my life anymore. Right now, wherever he is, whatever he needs, I ask you to work in his life and bless him.' And I still do that to this day.

"It's been a great release for me. It's been freeing for me. I don't hate him the way I used to."

I spoke to Rich again, some years later, on what happened to be the day after his latest visit to the doctor. Do you know what the doctor told him?

"Your guardian angel is looking over you."

"I'm healthy," Rich told me. "The doctor said my PSA levels are almost undetectable. He says everywhere he checked—my liver, my kidney, everywhere—he said things are going well.

"I needed healing in more than one area. Cancer Treatment Centers of America took care of the physical healing. I didn't really go to CTCA for emotional and spiritual healing, but I got that too. Forgiveness has helped me not only spiritually but also physically.

"Beyond the spiritual aspect of it, I now know that because I was able to forgive this person, I am definitely stronger physically, too. All the stress is out of my life, and my body is much more capable now to battle the cancer that was in me."

Chapter 6

SHARON

A Spontaneous Remission of Hatred

A spontaneous remission is the disappearance of cancer without any immediate medical cause. As my former employer, Memorial Sloan-Kettering President Lewis Thomas, MD, once said: "The rare but spectacular phenomenon of spontaneous remission of cancer persists in the annals of medicine, totally inexplicable but real, a hypothetical straw to clutch in the search for cure. . . . No one doubts the validity of the observation."

DR. RALPH MOSS, *THE MOSS REPORTS*

IT'S NO EASY THING TO watch a parent die. As Sharon Whitmore learned, it can be even harder to watch a parent suffer.

Sharon, now in her fifties, was the oldest daughter in a family of seven—five children and two working parents. She was raised to be a nurturer, caring for her brothers and sisters by cooking and cleaning. In many respects, she mothered them. It was especially hard, then, when her family was driven apart after her father sustained a brain injury in a horrific accident.

One morning in early 2008, Sharon's mother went to wake him and found him incoherent.

"She called the ambulance and they took him to the hospital. He had a massive hematoma in his brain, and it was inoperable. The doctor said that the prognosis was not good." They told the family that he would probably lose his ability to walk and would never again be able to function normally.

"He had a living will. It said not to do anything to keep him alive." But when it came down to it, Sharon's mother disagreed.

"It doesn't matter what the children think," her mother told the doctors, "it's what I think. I'm his wife and I say do whatever you can." Sharon argued, but her mother insisted: "I'll do what I want to do."

Sharon stormed out of the room and didn't return for several days. When she came back, she saw her father in a state of dependency that he'd never wanted.

"They had tubes everywhere. He had a feeding tube in his stomach, he had a catheter in him, he had a trache in him, he had a tube in his brain to drain blood." And it would only get worse. "He ended up getting a bedsore, and it got so bad that you could put your fist in it."

Sharon became angrier and angrier with her family for putting her father through increasing misery. "He had a living will and it was totally violated. I sat and watched as my father was cut apart, picked apart, and the anger just built up. He was so embarrassed because he knew his daughter was seeing him like that. It hurt me so badly because I knew how proud he was.

"You can imagine being a proud man and then having yourself brought to a level where people would take your covers off you and just leave you naked and exposed to your daughters," Sharon said. "I mean, the last thing he'd want is for his daughters to see him like that. It did a number on me."

In September 2008, Sharon's father passed away. She was diagnosed with cancer a short time later.

When she was told she had cancer, Sharon said, all she could think was, *My daddy's not here. He'd want to be with me; he'd want to help me because he loved me so much.*

"But I was blessed," she said. "I have a wonderful husband, and he supported me as I was faced with a decision: whether to have my breasts amputated with a mastectomy or to remove the mass. I opted for the removal and the treatment."

When the surgeons were unable to remove the entire mass, Sharon was devastated to learn that she would have to go back for a second operation.

"Any surgery is upsetting, and to take a part of a woman's body that actually makes her a woman is bad enough—but then to tell her that they have to go in and take more is even worse."

Her dissatisfaction with her first doctors led Sharon to Cancer Treatment Centers of America. She originally met with another member of my staff (along with the medical team), but found her way into my office one afternoon when he was unavailable. I asked about her cancer, and she told me something remarkable. She said she believed her cancer was caused by something within her heart.

"I never felt that way about anybody," she said, referring to her family. "And if I did, I would always pray for forgiveness; but this was something that I could feel festering in my soul."

"You know," I told her, "we have a program for forgiveness and it's not traditional—but it's one that I've found works. Are you willing to go through it?"

Without hesitation, she said, "Sure. Definitely, because I don't want this in me. I can't have this in me because I don't want cancer again, and I know that it was brought on from that."

"Do you feel that your cancer was caused by your anger with your family?" I asked her.

"Yes, I do," she said. "Yes, I do."

I asked Sharon if she wanted to move ahead with the program (she did), and if it was okay for me to pray with her (it was). I prayed for her, laying hands on her and anointing her with oil—which was, incidentally, exactly how her father used to pray for her.

"We had prayer," she would later say. "I mean, we had *prayer.*

At the time, I didn't realize it, but my heart truly wanted to forgive those people. I didn't want those negative feelings in me anymore. They were not *of* me. But I couldn't seem to do it. Every time I turned around, that's all I could talk about. Everybody I talked to, that's all I talked about. I mean, strangers, everybody. It just wouldn't go away."

But something happened. "When we finished praying, I felt a heaviness come off of me. But I didn't pay attention to it."

Instead, she went back to the rooms where she occasionally stayed during her visits to the hospital and sat down to work on her assignment.

"I started to write, and I wrote, 'These people did this to my father—' and I couldn't think of anything more. I couldn't *think*." Supposing she was just tired, Sharon lay down for a rest. When she got up, she tried to write for a second time.

"Nothing but gibberish came to my mind," she said. "Nothing. I was just sitting there thinking, *My gosh, what is wrong with me? This must be some kind of trick or something. This must be something Dr. Barry knows is going to happen to you*, because I still was not aware of what had actually happened."

Sharon stopped writing again, got a bite to eat, and then sat down for a third try at the assignment. As she sat staring at the blank sheet of paper, she realized that she had nothing to write; so she went to bed.

When she came back to my office the next day, she asked me, "What was that? I couldn't write anything. I tried to start and it was babble. When I left here, I just couldn't think. When I woke up this morning, it was the first day that I did not think about my father and what happened to him. Every morning, when I would say my prayers, I would just start crying about my dad—and this morning I didn't."

She said that, for the first time since her father's death, her heart didn't ache.

"Do you realize what happened?" I asked her. "Spontaneous remission."

Sharon had experienced with her forgiveness what doctors occasionally see with cancer and other physical ailments, when a tumor or disease unexpectedly and inexplicably disappears. There is no satisfying medical explanation for this phenomenon—people of faith (myself included) recognize it as a miracle.

The only reason that someone like Sharon, who was consumed by her anger and unforgiveness, might experience such an abrupt and instantaneous relief from her symptoms is through an act of God. Sharon wanted deliverance from anger and unforgiveness. When we prayed, it was removed from her.

"The writing out—I think it is the actual revelation of what is in you," she said. "When you write it down, you can see it and feel it. I couldn't write anything, because I had been delivered from it before I left the office.

"It was like a miracle. That's what it was like: it was like a miracle."

Of course, the process of forgiveness doesn't always happen so quickly, but that doesn't make Sharon's experience any less genuine, or her forgiveness any less life changing.

"They don't consider you cancer-free until it has been seven years now," Sharon said with a laugh, "but if I'm unforgiveness-free, I consider myself cancer-free."

The Science

We can no longer hide behind the argument that there is insufficient proof that mind/body methods have an impact or are effective. Studies indicate, in fact, the opposite is true.

DAVID SERVAN–SCHREIBER, MD, PHD
ANTICANCER: A NEW WAY OF LIFE (2009)

Chapter 7

THE BIOLOGY OF STRESS
Simplifying the Complex

Most of the diseases of abnormal immune function are
remarkably linked to psychological stress.
ROBERT SCAER, MD, *THE TRAUMA SPECTRUM*

Treating the whole person – mind, body, and spirit

About twenty-five years ago, during a lecture on the mind/body connection, one surgeon interrupted the presentation with a loud, "You don't seriously believe all this bull#@*%, do you?" Doctors, I have learned, have rules they live by: set procedures and "decision trees" established by evidence-based research (and insurance companies). As such, they wholeheartedly put their trust in the scientific method: is it measurable, predictable, and reproducible? However, God is not bound by their rules and continues to create new and improved ways of healing people, including awakening us to the reality of the role that the mind (our faith/belief system) can and does play in the healing process. Some physicians think more dynamically about healing and disease, and in doing so conclude: "When it comes to cancer, attitude is everything."[1]

Though not to everyone's satisfaction, attitudes toward holistic health care have certainly changed since the 1980s, to the point where the mind/body connection is now seen as "a perfectly respectable scientific hypothesis."[2] We have also come a long way since the early 1960s, when it was common for doctors not to tell patients that they even had cancer. Today's best treatments, by contrast, are modern, holistic, and patient-centered approaches to the disease. Old-school cancer treatments treated the tumor only. Newer cancer treatments treat the whole person—body, mind, and spirit.

Holistic cancer treatment is also called "integrative medicine," and it's the best cancer treatment available right now because, simply put, there is no silver bullet. There is no knockout punch that drops cancer to the mat, which isn't an easy thing to tell cancer patients or their friends and families. That's one reason, I suppose, that "fighting cancer" is the predominant metaphor when people speak about the disease: it really does require attacking it with everything you've got.

To underscore this point, Dr. Rudolph Willis, MD, chief of medical oncology at Cancer Treatment Centers of America in Philadelphia, relates a wisdom born from many years in the field of medical oncology when he says, "For some time, we cancer doctors have known that two different patients with the same cancer, with the same stage of the disease, and treated with the same therapy, might have completely different outcomes. One dies and the other doesn't. . . . There are innumerable frays in the battle for life, but the true war is fought by the most important warriors of all—one's spirit and one's faith."[3]

Dr. Willis understands the complexity of cancer in a way that few others can—but he also recognizes the role that patients play in their own healing. If you want your best chance to win in the fight against cancer, it is critically important to think dynamically about the disease, as well as to become more intimately aware of how and why our bodies do what they do. Those who value holistic health care seem to better appreciate the intricacies of the body (hormones, stress-related diseases, the role of nutrition, and the like) as well as the interrelatedness of its systems (e.g., the relationship between the endocrine and immune systems).

In short, holistic cancer treatment appreciates the complexity of the disease while recognizing the incredible resources that a patient can bring to the fight. Until a silver bullet is discovered—and we all hope that is soon—wise counsel dictates that cancer patients begin to think dynamically and treat holistically if the option is available.

A hospital program relating to forgiveness, then, fits well into the category of mind/body/spirit medicine. David Servan-Schreiber, MD, survivor of stage-IV brain cancer and author of *Anticancer: A New Way of Life* puts it this way: "The first step in [nurturing a patient's will to live] involves locating and treating past traumas."[4]

Why do you suppose he underscores the importance of treating past traumas first? Because the painful past is the genesis of disease? Yes! Servan-Schreiber goes on to say that "these poorly healed scars drain a significant portion of energy, and they hamper the body's capacity for self-defense."[5] Recent research has identified "a number of chronic health conditions . . . with social and interpersonal etiologies [causes or origins] and consequences. Forgiveness interventions offer important insights for management and treatment of these conditions."[6] Including cancer? *Absolutely*, according to Dr. Servan-Schreiber and many other researchers. Without a doubt.

The payoff

Before getting into the science of stress, we should answer one question right off the bat: *Why bother?* Why learn about stress, its effect on our bodies, and the role that forgiveness plays between the two?

The short answer is that there can be a huge payoff. The long answer may include any (or all) of the following examples:

1. *Forgiveness is a key to happiness.* "Forgiveness is the trait most strongly linked to happiness," writes University of Michigan

psychologist Christopher Peterson. "It's the queen of all virtues, and probably the hardest to come by."[7] Some people have been unhappy for so long they don't even remember what it feels like to be happy.

2. *Forgiveness heals painful memories and creates the opportunity for the healing of relationships.* For some people, the fabric of their family has been destroyed by painful memories of the past.

3. *Forgiveness offers "the way out."* Some people are sick and tired of being angry about the past and would make the effort to change their attitude if only they knew how.

4. *Forgiveness offers emotional, spiritual, and physical healing.* We might whisper to ourselves about another person, "You make me sick!" but we don't stop to think about the truth behind those words. Hating other people *does* make us sick.

5. *Forgiveness has an immediate, wholesome effect and long-term benefit.* The stress of unforgiveness affects the immune system negatively, as the ammunition that our bodies use to combat disease begins to run out. A strengthened immune system can positively affect healing from cancer.

If we're looking for a high rate of return, the possibilities presented by forgiveness offer an extremely high yield—perhaps more than any other process, when we consider the effort involved. The payoff is nothing short of personal peace—with others, ourselves, and possibly even with God. Its benefits are priceless.

But how does it all work?

THE SCIENCE OF STRESS

The connection between the mind and the immune system

Robert Ader, director of the Center for Psychoneuroimmunology Research in the department of psychiatry at the University of Rochester Medical Center, coined the term *psychoneuroimmunology*

(PNI) to describe the connection between the brain and the immune system.

PNI sounds awfully complicated until we break the word down to its component parts. The first part, *psycho*, relates to the mind, as in common terms such as *psychology, psychiatry,* and *psychic.* The second part, *neuro*, refers to *neurons*, which are the cells in the brain that relay electrical impulses, and has the same root as the word *nerve. Neuro* refers to the physical makeup of the brain, whereas *psycho* relates to the makeup of the mind. Finally, *immunology* is the science of the immune system.

Though researchers have yet to find "definitive evidence that psychosocial factors influence disease via changes in the immune system," Ader believes that "psychological experiences, such as stress and anxiety, can influence immune function, which in turn may have an effect on disease course."[8]

Certain data indicate that factors such as suppressing emotions of anger and hatred (which are the ingredients of unforgiveness) negatively influence a person's susceptibility to disease. But even though studies have begun to show a link between the mind and the immune system, Ader says, "if you're an immunologist and you read a lay magazine about how psychoneuroimmunology means you can boost your immune system and make you healthy, wealthy, and wise, you're not going to want any part of it."[9] His remarks are fair, and something we should keep in mind.

It is not the intent of this book to *overplay* the benefits of forgiveness as a "psychosocial therapeutic technique," but neither do I intend to *underplay* it. Forgiveness will not make you "healthy, wealthy, and wise," and I'm not suggesting it as a cure for all the world's problems. It is, however, a helpful way to cope with the stress created by hurtful emotional wounds that others have caused us—or that we have caused ourselves—with significant health benefits.

A commonsense observation about forgiveness as it relates to cancer is that unforgiveness, including the suppression of negative emotions, is very stressful. It takes a lot of energy to keep lavalike anger and hatred inside. Without a doubt, the retention of negative emotions is emotionally hard and toxic.

The stress response

What is *stress*—or, as it has become better known, the *stress response*? Does it affect the immune system; and, if so, how? More important, can stress cause the immune system to underfunction to the point that it either creates cancer or enhances tumor growth?

In order to answer these questions, we need to better understand the human endocrine system and its role in the secretion of hormones, which help the body to survive life-threatening situations. Everyone has strengths and weaknesses, things about their personalities that can either work for them or against them. The same is true at the molecular level. Hormones can help us; but if they are overused, they can also work against us.

What follows is a brief overview of the roles played by particular hormones that can affect a person's immune system as a response to stress. The science is far more complicated than our current discussion can fully explain, but I hope to at least shed some light on how our bodies can respond to unforgiveness.

The endocrine system

The endocrine system is one of the main communication systems for controlling and coordinating the body's work. It teams up with various other aspects of the body to maintain and control a whole host of functions, among which are body energy levels, homeostasis (the internal balance of body systems) and—most important for our purposes—the response to surroundings, injury, and stress.

The endocrine system accomplishes its work through hormones—chemical messengers, created and stored in the endocrine glands, that release molecular signals into the bloodstream when they're needed. We're all basically familiar with how the nervous system conveys information along neural pathways; similarly, the endocrine system uses the blood vessels to convey information throughout the body by way of hormones.

A brief word on hormones

The word *hormone* comes from the Greek *hormôn*, which literally means "to excite or spur on," which is exactly what hormones do. The human body has more than thirty of these amazing hormones busily orchestrating and regulating functions ranging from puberty and weight to how well we sleep and when we feel hungry or full. Furthermore, some hormones (two in particular) control how we handle stress. These are *adrenaline* and *cortisol*.

The function of adrenaline and cortisol is to generate strength and speed to survive a life-threatening situation, whether real or perceived. Specifically, adrenaline stimulates the heart to beat faster and stronger, in order to ensure strength and speed; while cortisol actively improves the brain's use of glucose and changes how we store energy. As a side note, these hormones are the reason that two simple lifestyle choices—exercise and increased water intake—can help reduce stress.

The fight or flight response

In order to increase the flow of blood to the brain and muscles—the organs that need it most in a life-threatening situation—adrenaline expands the blood vessels that feed these organs while constricting the blood vessels that feed other vital organs that have suddenly become less important. Cortisol also works to temporarily suppress unnecessary systems and bodily functions.

Let's say, for example, that we're enjoying a tranquil morning hike through the woods when an angry bear leaps out on the trail in front of us. Digesting the eggs and bacon we had for breakfast suddenly pales in importance to focusing our thoughts and preparing our legs for a high-speed chase through the underbrush. In such a situation, adrenaline and cortisol set us up for a period of sustained arousal that can help us survive the threat.

Along with suppressing the digestive system, the stress hormones also suppress the immune system. When confronted by the overwhelming and sustained threat of a bear breathing down our necks, cortisol marshals how our energy is spent and signals the immune system to significantly reduce production of NK cells, the body's foot soldier in the fight against cancer.

One researcher, Robert M. Sapolsky, says, "It is not that stress makes you sick, but that it increases the likelihood of contracting a disease that makes you sick. . . . In this scenario, stress-related disease arises because the defending army of the stress response runs out of ammunition."[10]

The net result is that our energy becomes focused on survival by addressing the most important threat: the bear. Fighting cancerous tumors and destroying cancer cells is important; but at the moment of stress, the bear presents a more immediate danger and thus eclipses even the need to fight cancer.

Here's the big problem: Our minds cannot distinguish between a real bear and an imaginary bear. To the extent that we see cancer, or any other problem, as a clear and present danger or threat, our bodies react accordingly, producing both adrenaline and cortisol, and yielding similar results: a body placed on high alert and ready for the fight of its life. However, as understandable as the concern may be, it is unhelpful to respond to the threat with overwhelming anxiety. A more helpful response would be to recognize the threat and, with faith and trust, calmly face the adversary. Cancer is not a "bear" that will destroy you; it is a disease that can be conquered.

Chronic stress

It isn't that stress in and of itself is bad. Our bodies have been created for stress. If we couldn't handle stress, we'd have to isolate ourselves from every other human being, becoming the type of person that Simon and Garfunkel immortalized in their song *I Am a Rock*: "Hiding in my room, safe within my womb, I touch no one and no one touches me."

Thankfully, God not only provided us the ability to experience productive, healthy stress, but he also designed our bodies to cope with external stressors—though only short-term ones. It would seem that God did not create us to maintain a state of hypervigilance in which our bodies would be continually flooded with stress hormones.

As an illustration, if our bodies are like cars, we have gas in the tank (glucose) and a gas pedal (endocrine system) to move us down the road. When we need to pass another car, or avoid one for whatever reason, we have a passing gear that dumps copious amounts of fuel into the carburetor, allowing us to move quickly around and away from the other car. But we were never intended to keep the gas pedal continually pressed to the floor.

Chronic stress is beyond God's design for our bodies; it is the subject of numerous Bible passages, most of which have to do with avoiding worry and fear, and encouraging trust and joy.

When I think of how intricately our bodies are made, I am reminded of and humbled by the words of the psalmist:

> For you created my inmost being;
> You knit me together in my mother's womb.
> I praise you because I am fearfully and wonderfully made;
> Your works are wonderful,
> I know that full well.[11]

STRESS, CANCER, AND MEMORY
Fight, flight, or . . . *freeze*

Much has been written about the fight-or-flight response. There is, however, a third option: *freeze*.

There's a true story about a lion that was chasing a zebra across the African plain. The zebra, running for its life, looked back to see if it had been able to outrun or outmaneuver the lion, only to find the predator closing in for the kill. The lion made a stretching swipe at the left hindquarter of the zebra, touching it ever so lightly, at which the zebra fell to the ground in a catatonic stupor, limbs limp, completely helpless, succumbing to the threat without continuing to struggle for life.

Some people view cancer as a similar threat. In fact, the diagnosis of cancer can trigger post-traumatic stress disorder (PTSD) in some people. Perceiving a cancer diagnosis as a death sentence, they sometimes give up without a fight, in much the same way as the zebra. Touched by the ultimate fear, they lie down and wait to die.

Robert Scaer, MD, author of *The Trauma Spectrum: Hidden Wounds and Human Resiliency*, writes, "Because helplessness is a state of reality or perception that is essentially required for the freeze response, one might also classify these medical syndromes as diseases of helplessness."[12] But freezing is at the extreme end of feeling helpless.

Last winter, I went skiing and snowmobiling with a good friend in the beautiful mountains of New Hampshire. I'm a fairly decent skier, but I haven't spent much time on a snowmobile. It was late in the season and the temperature was cool—not cold—and had been that way the prior week as well, making the snow a little soft, especially toward the side of the trail. I was following my friend, who was clipping right along and managing to stay at least twenty yards in front of me.

As I rounded a corner, I saw that he had stopped on the side of a very narrow trail. I froze in fear and momentarily blacked out. I still cannot remember the several seconds before I ran into the back of his snowmobile. Thankfully, no one was hurt, though I had obviously reached the point of extreme helplessness. In jest, I accused him of trying to kill me by stopping his snowmobile in front of me. But truth be told, even months later, it is still traumatic to think about the incident, leaving me to wonder how and why I could black out like that and under what circumstances it might happen again.

Although I can't explain what my neurons did during those fateful seconds, or how my brain, lungs, and other vital organs were functioning, I do understand what it's like to experience extreme helplessness, if only for a moment. Years earlier, I'd had a similar experience when I fell out of a boat, nearly costing me my life.

Experts suggest that successful treatment of PTSD involves helping the person discharge the experience of freezing. Some of the same techniques we use in our forgiveness program are also used in the treatment of PTSD. I'll come back to that later.

Painful memories: Sensory overload

One can't begin to address the healing of trauma without understanding our response to trauma as an *aberration of memory* that freezes us in a past event and thereafter dictates our entire perception of reality.[13]

Painful memories, it is important to note, consist of two parts: the pain itself and the memory. Picture a glass filled with cool, clear water. Imagine placing a drop of black ink into the water, creating a murky cloud. Now imagine that, through some sort of process of distillation, you can remove the ink from the water, creating clarity again.

Such is the process of forgiveness. The ink represents *pain* and the glass of water represents our *memory*. Successfully forgiving someone removes the pain from the memory, but the memory remains.

Because of the way our long-term memory works, we will probably never forget the situation that caused us pain; but that does not mean the pain must last forever. Like a scar on an arm or leg, we will never forget how the initial pain was created—whether it was by a broken glass, a fall off a bicycle, or in a kitchen fire—but the scar no longer hurts.

Figuratively, when someone hurts us emotionally, our hearts are wounded. Forgiveness allows the wounds to heal, but there will be scars. Though the wounds will heal, the memory remains. Forgiveness, then, is the healing of memory.

Ruminating about our past

Charlotte Witvliet, PhD, is a leading researcher in the field of forgiveness, particularly with respect to the physiology of forgiveness—or, to phrase it differently, how forgiveness and unforgiveness affect us physically. She writes:

In the wake of an offense, people often ruminate about the hurt, experience and express hostility toward the perpetrator, use hurtful strategies to cope with stress responses, and attempt to suppress one's negative emotions and feelings of vulnerability.

Unforgiveness draws people like magnets to ruminate about past hurts, embellish those narratives with bitter adjectives and adverbs that stir up contempt, exhibit avoidance and revenge motivations, cogitate about negative features of the offender and offense, and even rehearse a repertoire of grudge and revenge plots.[14]

Rumination is one of the ways that people attempt to understand what happened to them and why, as well as what life might have been like had they not been victimized. We often call this the What If? Game. These completely understandable thoughts often push the gas pedal of unforgiveness to the floor, sending a flood of stress hormones through our bodies, and giving credence to the conclusions offered by several researchers that unforgiveness is unhealthy. Dr. Everett Worthington, author of more than twenty-five books on forgiveness, writes, "Chronic unforgiveness causes stress. Every time people think of their transgressor, their body responds. Decreasing your unforgiveness cuts down on your health risk. Now, if you can forgive, that can actually strengthen your immune system."[15]

Until our memories are healed through forgiveness, we will continually be affected by what has happened to us. Even though the painful memory may not consciously come to mind, it doesn't mean it has gone away. Memories are waiting below the surface and can be triggered by many things. A New Yorker doesn't have to go very far or speak with many people in order to trigger memories of 9/11. The sight of snow can remind me of my snowmobile accident, and the sight of a lake or a ski boat quickly brings me back to my boating accident. A divorcée need only turn on the TV to find any number of triggers that can bring painful memories to the forefront.

I've noticed that cancer patients often suffer from "monkey mind"—you know, the tendency to jump around from this thought to that thought like so many branches in a tree—and often find it difficult to quiet their thoughts. Such are often easily distracted, and a monkey mind can prove fertile ground for negative thoughts to ruminate on the pain of the past. The word *ruminate* literally means "to chew the cud." Much like cows that chew their cud, we chew on past memories.

When we chew on our painful memories, they become a regular part of our consciousness. We often remember what happened—and how, or we try to figure out why it happened. We think about ways to get even and find joy in dwelling on the people who have hurt us—wishing them ill at best, and fantasizing about harming them at worst. But we only end up hurting ourselves in the process. Every time we revisit the person or event that caused us harm, we relive the experience emotionally, along with all the potentially harmful side effects.

Memories and metaphors

A word of caution about our memories: they are not as reliable as we might think. Contrary to popular perception, our memories are not like photographs, with details precisely captured, honestly portrayed, and easily recalled. Memory is more like a collection of impressionist paintings rendered by an artist who takes considerable license with the subject.

It's important to grasp the pliability of memory, because the memories we have (for the most part) have been laundered—they've been affected by perceptions, distorted by pain, and often caricatured to fit a scenario in which our own role is as positive as we can make it.

Why do we do this? In order to live with ourselves. No one wants to think badly of themselves, so we cook the books and reframe the picture in the most positive light possible. We all do it. It's an emotional survival technique that prevents us from doing more self-harm than we already do.

This explains, in part, why two children living in the same home can have very different memories about growing up. The same set of facts, seen from separate perspectives, are constantly being reframed and distorted, an impressionist painting in which truth is mixed with the paint of self-protection, making the memory of the event unrecognizable to others who were there.

Another factor to be considered, according to Dan Gilbert, author of *Stumbling on Happiness* (2005), is the way in which we store large amounts of memory. Memories are collapsed—think of large files on a zip drive—and then given a label, such as *Bad* or *Good*. Childhood is filled with a wide range of experiences, some good and some not so good. The mistake we often make is placing a label on fifteen years of experiences by referring to it as a *bad childhood*, when in reality there were plenty of good, happy experiences along the way.

Often when we work on forgiveness, the memory we are trying to heal is a distortion of what actually happened. The process of forgiveness, then, includes revisiting past situations or relationships to make sure that we are being truthful about what did or did not happen. Regardless of how we've distorted our memories, to the extent that they are painful, they need to be healed. The truth can—and will—set you free.

Time does not heal emotional wounds

Years ago, while I was serving in one of several churches in the South, I met a young woman, in her mid twenties, who was divorced and now married to a genuinely nice guy. In addition to our casual conversations, she had sought me out for counseling on several occasions. Every time we spoke, it was about the same thing: the way her first husband had sexually violated her. Although this had happened in her late teens, the topic came up in nearly every conversation with many people. She simply could not stop talking about it. In fact, in her role as one of our youth leaders, she finessed a way to speak about it to our youth group, under the guise of "date rape."

One of the biggest misconceptions about time is that it heals all wounds. The truth is that time does *not* heal all wounds, particularly deep wounds. The more severe the trauma, the less likely that the mere passage of time will be of much help at all. Over the years, James Pennebaker, professor of psychology at the University of Texas at Austin and author of *Opening Up: The Healing Power of Expressing Emotions*, has extensively explored the relationship between memory and emotions, as well as emotions and their effect on well-being—including their effect on the immune system. Though more will be said about Pennebaker's work in chapter 8, here is a brief introduction to his important research.

In one classic study, Pennebaker and his team sought to measure the benefit (if any) of writing about the traumas in one's life, which is often referred to as *narrative therapy*. Students in a freshman psychology class were sorted into three groups. One group, the control group, did not write about anything, creating a baseline. Another group was asked to write about whatever came to mind. The third group was asked to write specifically about their life's trauma, which was often related to their adolescent sexual trauma.

Over time, Pennebaker and his team correlated the information with the number of times each student got sick and went to the infirmary. Not surprisingly, the students who wrote specifically about their past trauma almost never got sick, whereas the control group—those who did not write at all—were the most frequently ill.

The conclusion reached by Pennebaker and his team—that withholding negative emotions correlates positively with suppressed immune function—has been the subject of many subsequent studies. For our purposes, it's clear that unforgiveness, at its core, is the withholding of negative emotions, such as anger, hurt, and hatred.

Some disclaimers

The initial research to correlate stress with the suppression of the immune system came from animal experimentation. In one such study, mice exposed to stressful situations showed a higher incidence of tumor growth. In fact, the noisier their environment, the faster their tumors grew. Another study exposed rats to electric shock in a variety of circumstances. Those without the ability to escape became lethargic and complacent, exhibited helplessness and a lack of desire, and lost their ability to resist cancer.

Is there a direct-line relationship between data like these and the effects of stress on humans? If you ask the researchers, you'll likely receive a nebulous response: maybe, maybe not.

One study in particular reported a link between major stressors and the onset of colon cancer in humans five to ten years later. But other researchers do not necessarily agree with the conclusions of that study. It makes for a situation that is both frustrating and limiting.

Let me be clear: when it comes to measuring the effects of stress in human subjects (regardless of whether the stress is induced in a laboratory by electric shock, or created naturally by unforgiveness) predictability of response will always vary. Part of what makes humans different from animals is our ability to think, reason, and ruminate about the past, as well as anticipate the future. Unfortunately for research on stress-related topics, people are different—they can and do make very different decisions based on the same information.

In working with my patients, who are all unique, I do not assume that what helped one person will help another. They each are seeking help, hope, and understanding—and, usually, a way out of an emotional and physical mess that has ensnared them. The counsel I offer is evidence based—that is, results drawn from rigorous research—but it is not a forgiveness pill they can take and then everything will be fine.

To the extent that stress and cancer are related, a silver bullet cure for cancer seems unlikely, simply because people respond differently to the same situations. We may have the same biological makeup, but beyond that, we all respond differently to various stressors: What makes one person cry makes another laugh; what makes one person lie down and die makes another stand and fight. The one consistent thing about us as humans is our inconsistency.

Even after accounting for age, sex, personality type, and other factors, the problem that continues to plague research involving human emotions—including our own forgiveness project—is predictability. The best we can do, it seems, is collect data through observation and clinical tests, analyze the facts as they are presented, and then make general conclusions based on rigorous assessment. In other words, we can narrow our conclusions, but we can't create a one-size-fits-all solution.

Additional problems arise from the difficulty in getting data from subjects, especially with respect to a cancer patient population. Long-term studies are difficult, because many of the patients do not survive their disease; short-term studies are often limited in scope, which leads to less-reliable conclusions.

Don't let a good hypothesis die

The engine that drives research of all kinds is *hypothesis*—that is, a theory or reasonable assumption—and that engine should not be allowed to run out of control. It should always be kept on track by skepticism, suspicion, and a willingness to test the results with reasonable questions. When it comes to researching a topic as unpredictable as human emotions—such as our forgiveness research—skepticism is often well warranted.

It's one thing to test a hypothesis, however, and quite another to ignore obvious conclusions, even though adequate proof seems elusive and absolute certainty unpredictable.

For example, studies have concluded that the overwhelming majority of breast cancer patients attribute their cancer to the effects of stress. Throughout this chapter, I offer compelling quotes from credible physicians and researchers that support these assertions; but can we absolutely prove there is a link? Some researchers would say yes, and others no. Does that make those battling breast cancer wrong? They know their bodies—before, during, and after the disease—but drawing a definitive line between stress and cancer remains difficult.

When we add to the mix the role of chronic stress created by suppressing or withholding negative emotions (which is the essence of unforgiveness), the additional variable makes it quite difficult to draw conclusions. And quite frankly, those conclusions may never be proven to the level of a skeptic's satisfaction. Nevertheless, we shouldn't let a good hypothesis die at the hands of overeager skepticism.

Herb Benson, MD, proves the point when he says, "Sixty to 90 percent of visits to physicians are for conditions related to stress. Harmful effects of stress include anxiety, mild and moderate depression, anger and hostility, hypertension, pain, insomnia, and many other stress-related diseases."[16]

Dr. Benson is highly credentialed and well respected, particularly in the circles of mind/body medicine. When he says 60 to 90 percent of doctor visits are stress related, it sounds impressive and convincing, but not very precise. What we can glean, however, is that stress appears to make a lot of people sick. If that's the point, I'm 100 percent sure he's right.

If I want a high quality of life

This book is not primarily about stress or cancer or God. Instead, it's a primer about personal peace gained through forgiveness, and a study of the influence of forgiveness on relationships. In closing this chapter, I'll tell you the same thing I tell my patients: I'm fifty-eight years old, and I'm not going to make it to 158. Neither will you. Death awaits us all. But I am committed to enjoying my life until my final breath. I am determined to drink the last drop from the cup of life. And if I should find myself trudging through an emotional tar pit of anger and hatred, I will do whatever I can to free myself from the messy goo so that I can live the joyful life that God intends for me. I may not live forever in my earthly body, but I can make choices about how I live. One thing I've decided is that I refuse to be angry at others, including God. Forgiveness is the key that unlocks the door.

Chapter 8

CANCER AND EMOTIONAL TRAUMA

Inwardly, the emotional wound also affects deep vital processes. . . . A psychological wound sets off mechanisms of the stress response: release of cortisol, adrenaline, and inflammatory factors, as well as a slowdown in the immune system. . . . These physiological stress mechanisms can contribute to the growth and spread of cancer.

DAVID SERVAN-SCHREIBER, MD, PHD,
CANCER AND THE EMOTIONAL WOUND

FOLLOWING COMPLETION OF our forgiveness program, one of my patients, Linda, wrote me a letter.

Rev. Barry,

For the past several years, I have been carrying around many negative feelings for certain people in my life. I knew this was detrimental to my life, but I did not know how to deal with it. After meeting with you last week, I did as you said. I kept a journal of my feelings. Over a period of two days, I wrote in my journal three times for a period of twenty minutes each time. I started out bitter and angry, went on to see the individual[s] as [people], and began to resolve my feelings and forgive them for what they had done to me.

I was amazed at the freedom I experienced by letting go of the hurt. Once I looked at forgiveness from a different perspective, I understood that, just as we want God to forgive us, we must forgive others. [When I wouldn't forgive] people, they were not being punished. I was. I was being kept prisoner of my own negative emotions. In forgiving them, I freed myself. What a fabulous concept!

All this energy can now be used for healing my mind, spirit, and body. This is a much more positive use of energy. I want to thank you and your staff for all the support you have shown me. . . .

Sincerely,

Linda

Linda's testimony answers the question, Is there a relationship between cancer and unforgiveness? with an unequivocal *yes*.

Robert Scaer, MD, in his seminal work *The Trauma Spectrum*, affirms that the endocrine system—and the hormone cortisol in particular—is closely linked with the immune system: "High levels of cortisol inhibit immune responses. Most diseases of abnormal immune function are remarkably linked to psychological stress."[1] Dr. Scaer's observation is corroborated by Dr. Donald P. Braun, PhD, the vice president of Clinical Research for Cancer Treatment Centers of America.[2] Dr. Braun observes:

The most profound effect on anyone who's experienced a forgiveness intervention is a feeling of peace, a feeling of letting go of things that they may have been carrying around for most of their life. What would the physiologic consequences of that be? Certainly a remarkable reduction in anxiety, a remarkable reduction in those hormones and mediators that influence psychological states like depression. We know that patients who have experienced the kind of peace that forgiveness interventions can produce are going to have less problems with nausea, less problems with difficulties in healing their wounds, and . . . a better capacity to fight their cancer with their immune system. And it also means that if we can control the anxiety levels and the cortisol levels in the blood of patients, we expect that their bone marrow recovery will be more robust.[3]

Beyond helping people in active treatment for cancer, consider life *after* cancer. Braun notes:

One of the things that we are committed to doing in our patients is *preparing them to be survivors*. We know that when the treatment is finished, many of our patients are going to be cured or they're going to enjoy long periods of remission from their cancer. Therefore, we need to prepare their bodies to be able to resist the recurrence of their cancer in any way we can.[4]

The latest research has yielded this conclusion:

Over an extended period of time, unforgiveness can be experienced as negative emotions that result in a cascade of biological and brain responses. Findings about the body's hormone response to unforgiveness reveal that unforgiveness is reflected in specific cortisol levels, adrenaline production, and cytokine balance . . . , with patterns that parallel those reported in people living with high stress. These hormone patterns are known to compromise the immune system . . . with the long-term consequence of leading to several identified chronic illnesses.[5]

It is reasonable to conclude that, to the extent unforgiveness creates psychological stress through the withholding of negative emotions, the immune system is suppressed, which leads to negative health consequences, including the possibility of cancer.

As we know, unforgiveness involves ruminating about painful memories. This creates a cascade of very predictable activities at the physical level (at the spiritual level too, but I'll address that in a later chapter), often because we *feel* helpless and disempowered. But we're not.

We feel helpless and disempowered either because we are *not motivated* to forgive, for various reasons, or because we *do not know how* to forgive. Either way, we find ourselves trapped by our own lack of desire for zestful living, addicted to the emotional rush created by vengeful thoughts, or lacking in the knowledge necessary to escape our painful memories—and oftentimes, all three.

Over time, the waterfall of hatred and anger will cause "physiologic weathering"—the erosion of body, mind, and spirit. A constant flood of adrenaline and cortisol can and will affect the cardiovascular system, creating the possibility of heart disease. It can and will keep you from being the happiest person you can be. It can and will inhibit the development of close relationships. It can and will cause your immune system to underfunction, creating a good possibility of bad things happening to your body. It can lead to a shortened life span.

This is similar to smoking cigarettes, which may not give you cancer, but the full list of negative consequences is worth noting. Smoking increases the risk of

- lung cancer
- other lung diseases, such as emphysema
- other cancers, such as cancer of the mouth, cervix, and bladder
- heart disease
- stroke
- ulcers

- hip fractures
- sleep disorders
- more frequent development of colds and other respiratory infections

A person may smoke for decades and never get cancer. Similarly, a person may be filled with anger and never contract disease. But, in light of what we know about the relationship between smoking, lung cancer, and ancillary diseases, it doesn't make sense to smoke. The same is true with harboring anger and hatred, with choosing not to forgive.

The choice between unforgiveness and forgiveness may not be the choice between apathy, indifference, and laziness on the one hand, and happiness and passionate living on the other. But the biology of stress suggests that there are better ways to live. Coping mechanisms can be employed and skill sets can be developed—*if* what you want is to live a healthy, well-balanced life.

A closer look at the word *medicine* might be helpful. Its root word is *med*, which is the Latin equivalent of the English *mid*, from which we get the word *middle*. When we are feeling out of balance, we go to the doctor, who prescribes medicine to bring us back to a state of homeostasis, equilibrium, and balance—*back to the middle*. I went for my annual physical exam the other day and learned that I need to increase my vitamin D levels substantially. Lower levels lead to fatigue. It isn't easy to maintain balance in life, but the consequences of living an unbalanced life are not compelling. I hope you agree that the effort required to live a balanced life, though sometimes difficult, is an effort worth making.

What is forgiveness?

Before continuing our discussion of unforgiveness, we should address a different question altogether: what is *forgiveness*?

Answering that question is a little like describing chocolate cake to someone who's never eaten cake. A simple answer like "it tastes sweet" doesn't describe the cake or fully explain the experience;

multiple descriptions are required, and even those pale when compared to biting into a piece of chocolate decadence. So it is when defining forgiveness.

The biblical answer is that forgiveness is *the canceling of a debt*,[6] but this raises more questions than it answers and is as unsatisfying as it is simple. Words can never completely describe forgiveness and the emotional experience attached to it.

Forgiveness is a *one-sided emotional transaction* in which the canceling of a person's debt results in a heartfelt sense of peacefulness for the person who forgives. There is a paradoxical element to forgiveness, in that "as an individual lets go of his or her anger, hatred, or the need for revenge, it is they who are healed," writes Barbara Elliott.[7]

To put it another way, forgiveness is being able to wish someone well and truly mean it, even though we may never want or need to see that person again. Forgiveness does not require us to like someone. To be sure, some people are so incredibly toxic that they are completely unlikable and, for our own sake, we should not see them again. Jayne, for example, worked very hard to forgive the men who abducted her husband—but she never has to face them again. Rich may never again speak to his cousin.

You may never again see the person who harmed you, but that doesn't mean you can't find it in your heart to silently whisper these words to yourself: "I wish you well with your life, and I hope and pray you will cause no more damage to me or anyone else. Go in peace."

The person who can speak those words

- understands that harm has been done;
- is not excusing or trivializing it;
- refuses to be consumed with anger or thoughts of revenge; and
- leaves the righting of wrongs in the hands of those who have the responsibility for mediating justice.

That is forgiveness in its essence.

I heard a sermon recently in which the pastor told a story about one of his favorite childhood games, Time Bomb. Time Bomb is a game in which a big plastic "bomb" is wound up and begins ticking. The idea is to pass the ticking ball around the circle with the hope that it will explode while someone else is holding it.

Isn't it fun to watch someone else "explode"? When someone hurts us, we often want to get even by hurting them back. We *want* them to explode!

Forgiveness, however, does not mean taking someone's harmful act and keeping the hurt and pain inside yourself, which is like holding on to the Time Bomb. Neither does it mean throwing it back to the other person—which is what most of us want to do, or passing it off to someone else, which is the nature of pain—it affects those closest to us. Rather, we should defuse the Time Bomb with an act of love. Don't pass it back. Don't pass it off. Defuse it with forgiveness, so that it doesn't hurt you or anyone else.

Locking antlers

Some male deer, during mating season, will butt heads and accidentally lock their antlers together. Unable to disentangle themselves, both bucks will end up dying, either from exhaustion or dehydration. How many of us lock antlers with others, to the point that we end up causing great harm to ourselves? It doesn't make sense, but it happens all the time. Unfortunately, we can remain emotionally locked to those who have hurt us long after we have become physically separated.

Forgiveness is best understood as a process that begins with a decision to forgive the perpetrator of harm, and ends with an emotional release of the anger or hatred. You'll know you have arrived when the anger and hatred is replaced by a feeling of peaceful indifference or neutrality.

The emotion of forgiveness is similar to the feeling we might have toward people we have never met; quite simply, if we don't know them, there is no reason to hate them or be angry with them. We would treat them with common decency and respect. If a stranger were to drop a pencil, most people would likely bend down, pick it up, and return it without ever developing an attraction or fondness for the person. The Greek word for this kind of feeling is *phileo*, from which we get the word Philadelphia, the city of brotherly love. I believe this is what Jesus had in mind when he spoke of forgiveness from the heart (Matthew 18:35).

The goal of forgiveness, therefore, is to replace toxic feelings of hatred with the more life-giving, nonlethal, neutral feeling of love. This feeling is born out of a well-meaning, peaceful indifference that allows us to wish the best—and mean it—for those who have harmed us.

What is unforgiveness?

In George Macdonald's *Unspoken Sermons* (1867), he writes, "It may be an infinitely less evil to murder a man than to refuse to forgive him. The former may be the act of a moment; the latter is the heart's choice."

Unforgiveness, then, is the opposite of peaceful indifference or forgiveness from the heart. It is a state of mind that represents anger, vengeance, and hatred toward the person who has harmed us. It is a state of being in which the victim, for a number of possible reasons, remains emotionally stuck, entangled in a web. While trapped in this web, negative feelings are suppressed and attention shifts from more positive emotions (such as happiness and joy) to ruminating about past hurts, which serves as a source for chronic stress.

From a secular standpoint, forgiveness yields health benefits through the healing of painful memories. From a religious standpoint, forgiveness helps to restore peace with God and our fellow man. As the Muslim scriptures teach:

He who forgiveth, and is reconciled unto his enemy, shall receive his reward from God; for he loveth not the unjust doers.[8]

The Bible puts it this way:

> If anyone says, "I love God," yet hates his brother, he is a liar; for he who does not love his brother, whom he has seen, cannot love God, whom he has not seen.[9]

Forgiveness, then, is considered the right thing to do by many—if not most—of the world's religions. Regardless of the health benefits, it is a highly valued aspect of faith.

Is there a relationship between cancer and *un*forgiveness?

Is there a relationship between cancer and unforgiveness? I believe there is; research confirms the relationship, and my patients would agree, as their testimonials have shown. Here is what can be said with 100 percent accuracy, based on both my experience and credible research:

1. Unforgiveness does not *cause* cancer.
2. Forgiveness will not *cure* cancer.
3. Stress does not cause cancer, but how one copes with stress through lifestyle decisions (such as alcohol use, smoking, the suppression of negative emotions, and other at-risk behaviors) is highly correlated to various diseases, including cancer.
4. Unforgiveness involves the suppression of negative emotions.
5. Suppression of negative emotions can develop into a state of chronic stress.
6. Chronic stress can disable the body's ability to defend itself from diseases.
7. Many of my patients have experienced renewed personal peace, or a "feeling of lightness," and believe it has had a positive effect on their ability to battle their disease.

Each of the people whose stories I've told would attest to their belief that their hatred led, in no small way, to their disease. Based on the research I have shared, I have no reason to doubt their beliefs or intuition. After all, they know their bodies better than anyone else.

Recall Jayne's experience: "I felt an enormous wave of relief, as if the weight of the world had just been lifted from my shoulders. It was amazing. I felt so much lighter." Moreover, and much to Jayne's surprise, she felt the most relief in the very places in her body where she had the disease. "I had gotten it off my chest," she smiled. "Literally."

Certainly, Jayne's experience created an internal emotional shift; and however anyone else might characterize her experience, it was life changing for her.

If my patients tell me, then, that their internalized anger and hatred has health consequences, who am I (or anyone else) to argue with their self-assessment? Especially when their self-assessments correlate well with the opinion of researchers such as Keith J. Petrie, Roger J. Booth, and James Pennebaker, who write, "A personal coping style that suppresses emotion may increase the risk of cancer."[10] As we've seen, unforgiveness suppresses negative emotions.

Other bioscientists and forgiveness researchers, on the other hand, may not be so quick to agree. Their reasons lie within the construct of the scientific method: is it measurable, predictable, and reproducible?

There is nothing about Jayne's story that is measurable, predictable, or reproducible. Neither, for that matter, are the experiences of the others I have shared with you.

Nevertheless, is there a baseline of information that unarguably proves the connection between *unforgiveness* and *health consequences*? The answer is *yes*. But is there a baseline of information that provides the connection between *unforgiveness* and *cancer*? In all fairness to the demands of research scientists and those requiring hard data, the answer is *probably*.

My answer, on the other hand, is *yes*.

I have made, and continue to make, my case using available data, the wisdom of other experts, and common sense. It has become a balancing act—maintaining my credibility as a researcher while taking seriously the beliefs and experiences of my patients (not to mention my own personal experiences of forgiveness and religious beliefs).

Forgiveness researchers Alex H. S. Harris and Carl E. Thoresen tell us that "the notion that unforgiveness is linked to health risks is a small leap. Yet the devil may be in the details."[11] But I have also learned that God is in the details, and this becomes most obvious when truth is encountered.

Details, combined with powerful if not miraculous experiences of changed lives, may not be enough to convince some skeptics. I'll let you decide for yourself. But while you are deciding, here's something to keep in mind: "Like every facet of the body's physiology, the continuum between optimal, normal, and impaired function is subtle. So too, the line between health and disease is a fine one."[12]

Who knows where the line is drawn between surviving cancer and not surviving cancer. Is there a point at which the disease crosses the line from survivability to certain death? Is there a point in a cancer patient's journey where he or she faces the proverbial fork in the road? A point at which, if this therapy or that is tried, the outcome may be better? Or significantly better? Where exactly is the line between those who will survive and those who will not?

Wherever the line is drawn, forgiveness is one more helpful step in the journey to get over the line, beat the disease, and join the ranks of long-term survivors.

Recent conclusions of forgiveness research

Christina M. Puchalski, MD, is the founder and director of the George Washington Institute for Spirituality and Health and assistant professor at the George Washington University School of Medicine. In one of her helpful articles, she sums up the latest research on unforgiveness by identifying some common characteristics of unforgiving people:

- increased anxiety symptoms
- increased paranoia

- increased narcissism
- increased frequency of psychosomatic complications
- increased incidence of heart disease
- less resistance to physical illness
- increased incidences of both depression and callousness toward others[13]

Furthermore, she writes that the act of forgiveness results in

- less anxiety and depression,
- better health outcomes,
- increased coping with stress, and
- increased closeness to God and others.[14]

Here are some of the conclusions reached by other researchers:

Forgiveness was also found to be *significantly related to critical health behaviors*. Of the 91 [HIV/AIDS] patients who were prescribed antiretroviral medications, feeling unforgiven by important others was associated with significantly more missed doses of medication in the previous week.[15]

Translation: The feeling of unforgiveness can lead to poor self-care, which can lead to poor health outcomes. Hatred, including self-hatred, often finds its target and it hurts us at many levels.

By helping patients manage not just their disease but also common underlying needs for spiritual meaning, including forgiveness, *quality of life as well as health outcomes for the self and loved ones* can be markedly improved and at significantly lower costs than when medical interventions alone are used.[16]

Translation: Treating issues related to both body and soul enhance quality of life and reduce health costs. Triaging emotional wounds through forgiveness interventions have proven to be a helpful part of this process.

> Unforgiveness might be linked to poor health outcomes through the consequence of *problematic coping styles, such as avoidance coping or substance use.*[17]

Translation: Forgiveness is an extremely important coping mechanism. In other words, being able to forgive helps us cope with some of the bumps and grinds that life throws at us. Without the willingness or capacity to forgive, we may survive the ordeal but not thrive.

Dr. Stephen Locke, from Harvard Medical School, did a study in which he compared people who had high stress and low coping mechanisms to those who had both high stress and high coping mechanisms. His research concluded that those with high coping mechanisms produce *three times* the number of NK cells, which serve as the frontline defenders against invading cancer cells.

According to Locke, "the negative impact of stress on the immune system can apparently persist over several years of repression or suppression of emotion. In one study, more than forty years after the Holocaust, the act of verbalizing the experience resulted in significantly fewer doctor's visits and fewer reports of health problems among survivors during the next year, particularly for those whose narratives used the most emotional words."[18]

> Clinically, it is important to consider forgiveness in relation to the various kinds of strategies people use to cope with the stress of unforgiveness. People who suppress [their emotions], binge, smoke, misuse alcohol and other substances, aggress, withdraw, and ruminate to manage unforgiveness will engage with known links to adverse health outcomes.[19]

Translation: Forgiveness is more than a coping mechanism or strategy, but it is at least that. Forgiveness offers opportunities to better manage the emotions created by painful experiences and their memories, and emotional management is often a key to successful cancer treatment.

Sir Peter Medawar, the great British scientist and Nobel Prize winner in immunology, was once asked what the best prescription against cancer might be. "A sanguine personality," he replied.[20] Sanguine is a word that means *cheerful* or *hopefully optimistic*, and it correlates to positive emotions such as joy and happiness. If the best treatment for cancer is a more cheerful disposition, then unforgiveness may be what keeps us from finding peace. Unforgiveness sabotages our best efforts to find healing and hope.

It is fairly obvious that the ability to cope well with a painful memory is connected to externalizing the negative feelings and experiences. Continually suppressing negative feelings negatively affects immune function. In other words, it is not whether we experience a lot of stress (forgiveness-related or otherwise), but how we choose to cope with it.

It must be said, however, that forgiveness may be the *best* coping mechanism we know about.

Forgiveness research at Cancer Treatment Centers of America, Inc.

As director of pastoral care at a prestigious cancer treatment hospital, I see patients every day who have had, in many cases, very hard lives. Cathy, whose story is told in chapter 4, was one of them. These patients often discuss with me their life's problems. Too often, their problems take the form of unresolved anger and bitterness, usually related to their experiences with friends and relatives. My observations and concerns led me to conduct a formal study on forgiveness as it relates to cancer patients.

The nuances of cancer research

In scientific research, one rule-of-thumb is that *the bigger the better*. The more people surveyed, the more credible the research results in the eyes of other researchers and the general public.

Further, *the longer the better.* The longer the period of data acquisition, the more likely its conclusions will be considered as reasonable and valid. For example, a study of 50,000 people over a three-year period is likely to be taken more seriously than one with fifty people over a six-month period.

However, the very nature of cancer treatment often precludes lengthy studies, for reasons not readily apparent to those unfamiliar with the landscape of cancer treatment.

For one thing, the overwhelming majority of cancer patients, at least at CTCA, receive *outpatient* treatment, which means it is common for a patient to arrive at 8 a.m. for a chemotherapy treatment and be gone by 10 a.m., if not sooner. Outpatient cancer treatment has an often unpredictable and rapid flow: moments of prolonged waiting followed by a rush to various providers, treatment, and then home. Sometimes, simply locating a patient is very difficult, much less conducting an in-depth discussion about forgiveness—even as important as that discussion may be to both the patient and me. The second hindrance to long-term forgiveness research, unfortunately, is that not all of our patients survive the disease.

Therefore, our team decided to intentionally scale a research project that would be shorter and smaller than we might otherwise prefer, yet still big enough and long enough to test some of our hypotheses and provide credible results. We do not assume that our project is anything other than a serious attempt to better understand the needs of our patients, with the ultimate goal to increase the quality of their lives, equip them emotionally to fight their disease, and increase their immune function.

Our project

Our research was guided by four foundational assumptions:

1. Repression of negative emotions (such as those created by unforgiveness) creates stress, which in turn has a potentially negative effect on immune system function.

2. Cancer patients often suppress negative emotions (see Type-C personalities).
3. Cancer patients frequently speak of issues related to interpersonal forgiveness with pastoral care chaplains.
4. Therefore, forgiveness interventions would especially benefit cancer patients.

For a year and a half, our pastoral care team inquired about attitudes related to forgiveness during our thirty-minute new patient orientation program, which included a brief spiritual assessment form. One question on the form asked about the patient's perceived need to forgive prior health care professionals, God, themselves, or others. **Thirty-nine percent of our patients self-identified forgiveness issues, and approximately half of those respondents expressed *high* to *severe* forgiveness concerns in their lives.**

These results were not surprising; in fact, to a great degree, they confirmed what we had already suspected. However, from a *formal research* perspective, the results weren't helpful, because of the method we used to collect the data. Compliance with strict governmental research standards would have required us to use a survey that was both anonymous and voluntary to gather the information. **When we used an anonymous/voluntary survey, the percentage of our patients who self-identified forgiveness issues increased significantly to sixty-one percent, and approximately half of those expressed *high* to *severe* forgiveness concerns in their lives.**

From this information, we drew several conclusions:

1. Sixty-one percent of our cancer patients suffer from unforgiveness.
2. Thirty-four percent of our patients suffer from high to severe forgiveness-related issues.
3. A high percentage of our patients are unwilling to openly admit during an initial evaluation that they struggle with forgiveness issues.

It may or may not surprise you that only a small percentage of patients seek forgiveness-related programs; most prefer to maintain the status quo and continue their journey while silently holding onto their anger and refusing to forgive.

Reflecting on the data triggered a comment from one of my pastoral care colleagues, the Rev. Robin Childs, who recalled his experience in conducting new patient orientation meetings. In discussing the forgiveness question on our NPO Spiritual Assessment Questionnaire (which is different from our survey), Robin noted the frequency with which patients had told him they *used to have* forgiveness issues with people, but had *already forgiven them*. The rest of the team nodded in agreement. That statement was a very common response, but it had largely gone unnoticed in our attempts to identify patients who *did* struggle with forgiveness issues.

Keeping in mind that many of our patients have been battling cancer for years, it seems perfectly plausible that the diagnosis of cancer, along with its potentially life-threatening prospects, would trigger many to do something they knew they should have done— but hadn't—*before their diagnosis*: rid themselves of their anger and hatred by forgiving those who had hurt them.

We may conduct further research to better understand our data, but our team is confident that many of our cancer patients would say: "Don't wait until you have cancer to forgive those who have hurt you!"

Each patient who goes through our forgiveness program seems to know, deep down, that forgiveness is important. Many find the peace they are seeking. They seem to sense that there's a relationship between their disease and the unforgiveness they have been harboring. After experiencing forgiveness, they are all the more convinced of it.

There are only two options available for people who have experienced emotional wounds: they can leave their pain in the past, or they can continue to carry it with them. If they want to leave it in the past, so that their memories are no longer painful, then they have no other option but to forgive the people who have harmed them.

What is it going to take?

We've explored the meaning of stress and its relationship to immune function. We've carefully considered its relevancy to forgiveness and investigated the concept of unforgiveness. And in the spirit of leaving no stone unturned, I've invited you to consider forgiveness as a transaction in which the gain/loss ratio is markedly in favor of those willing to take the risk of forgiving. The payoff leads to a rebalanced life.

In the face of all the evidence presented thus far, the question remains: Why don't more people pursue forgiveness as a beneficial practice in their lives? After all, there are no research results to suggest that cancer patients have more forgiveness issues than the rest of the population.

But as psychologist Edwin Friedman once said, "The unmotivated are notoriously invulnerable to insight."[21]

So, what does it take to motivate people to forgive? That's the question we'll attempt to answer in the next chapter.

The Problem

The colossal misunderstanding of our time is the assumption that insight will work with people who are unmotivated to change.
EDWIN H. FRIEDMAN, *FRIEDMAN'S FABLES*

Chapter 9

IN SEARCH OF MOTIVATION
What Is Avoidance?

Avoidance is a common reaction to trauma. It is natural to want to avoid thinking about or feeling emotions about a stressful event. But when avoidance is extreme, or when it's the main way you cope, it can interfere with your emotional recovery and healing.
LAURA E. GIBSON, PHD, "AVOIDANCE"
NATIONAL CENTER FOR POST-TRAUMATIC
STRESS DISORDER FACT SHEET

I DIDN'T ACTUALLY think about writing a book on forgiveness until about five years ago. I reviewed the available literature and found that, at the time, all roads seemed to lead through four researchers, one of whom was Fred Luskin, author of *Forgive for Good*. He also serves as director of the Stanford Forgiveness Project, which studies the effectiveness of his research programs with people who have experienced the violence in Northern Ireland, Sierra Leone, and the 9/11 World Trade Center attacks.

Stepping out on a limb, I Googled Dr. Luskin's bio, dialed his number at Stanford, and—*Eureka!*—he answered the phone. He couldn't have been more congenial as I shared my interest in the topic of forgiveness and told him that I was considering writing a book on the topic. Although he wasn't discouraging (okay, maybe a little), he said something I'll never forget, something that has rung true over my many years of working on forgiveness with patients: "There is no need for another book on forgiveness. What needs to be written is a book motivating people to want to forgive."

Of course, as a Christian pastor, my immediate thought was, *Well, that book has already been written: it's called the Bible.* And though that's true, the question remains—and it still haunts me: *Why are people not more motivated to forgive?* Why aren't there more people whose passion for healthy living drives and empowers them to seek to engage in forgiveness programming? Why aren't more people like the Amish, who seem to embrace forgiveness as a way of life? It's almost as if they operate by different rules than the rest of us.

The problem, as it turns out, is *avoidance*, a very common symptom of people who have been and continue to be traumatized by the memory of painful experiences.

Much of my research over the past five or six years has been an attempt to create an effective curriculum for those who have already found the motivation to forgive; but I continue to ponder the seemingly unanswerable question of why people aren't more motivated to forgive, even after they learn about the health consequences of unforgiveness and the spiritually deadening impact of holding on to anger and hatred.

When it comes to many of the most important questions in life—such as why some people survive their disease while others succumb, or why some prayers seem to be answered while others aren't—we all stand before the great mystery. No one, not even the best physicians or theologians in the world, can satisfyingly answer those questions.

Don't get me wrong. I have formulated some answers, and on occasion they seem to be pretty good ones; but in the face of human tragedy and unanswered prayers, most answers, including my own, are unsatisfying. Ancient wisdom teaches us:

> "For my thoughts are not your thoughts,
> neither are your ways my ways,"
> declares the LORD.
> "As the heavens are higher than the earth,
> so are my ways higher than your ways
> and my thoughts than your thoughts."[1]

Certain things in life will elude our knowledge and understanding, regardless of our efforts to explain them. The more we learn about something, the more there seems to be an expanding universe of more questions.

One of the more mysterious questions I face on a daily basis has to do with human motivation; that is, what does it take to get people to do what they know they need to do? To eat well, or exercise on a regular basis. To even do something as basic as being willing to fight for their own lives. People are mysterious, and perhaps what motivates them is as mysterious as they are.

A simple Google search of "Motivational Theories" yielded the following academic theories about motivation, among others:

- *Acquired Needs Theory*: We seek power, achievement, or affiliation.
- *Affect Perseverance*: Our preferences persist even after being invalidated.
- *Attitude-Behavior Consistency*: Our attitudes and behaviors are more likely to align if several factors are true.
- *Attribution Theory*: We need to attribute cause to events around us in a way that supports our ego.
- *Cognitive Dissonance*: Nonalignment is uncomfortable, so we seek alignment.
- *Cognitive Evaluation Theory*: We select tasks based on how doable they are.

- *Consistency Theory*: We seek the comfort of internal alignment.
- *Control Theory*: We seek to control the world around us.
- *Disconfirmation Bias*: We agree with what supports our beliefs and are critical of what doesn't.
- *ERG Theory*: We seek to fulfill needs of existence, related-ness, and growth.
- *Escape Theory*: We seek to escape uncomfortable realities.
- *Goal-Setting Theory*: We are motivated by goals that are clear, challenging, and achievable.[2]

Add to this list Maslow's Hierarchy of Needs, and all we can do is shake our heads and wonder if we will ever be able to understand why we do what we do—or, more to the point, why we don't do what we know we should do.

Deep within our human DNA is a very conflicted and confused double helix that consistently manifests itself in self-contradiction and self-sabotaging behavior. We often are not motivated to do the very thing we know we could and should do, and vice-versa. The Bible bears witness to this phenomenon through the teachings of the apostle Paul, who writes, "I have the desire to do what is good, but I cannot carry it out. For what I do is not the good I want to do; no, the evil I do not want to do—this I keep on doing."[3]

Why do people do what they do? Perhaps some of the following ideas will stimulate you to engage in the most important action required of humans: *forgiveness*.

No regrets

Of the many subtle, internal nudges that move me into action, none has been more effective than the feeling of *regret*. Fear is a powerful motivator too, but it comes second to regret. I couldn't begin to explain the depth of its influence over me, but I know that, over a lifetime of decision making, regret—or the desire to avoid regret—has usually been the determining factor in what I've chosen to do or not do.

I try to live my life without regrets, as I'm sure you do. It probably has something to do with my desire for integrity—the desire to have my actions match my words. Poets and philosophers have captured this idea, though perhaps none better than Sydney J. Harris: "Regret for the things we did can be tempered by time; it is regret for the things we did not do that is inconsolable."[4]

The Rev. Dr. Bryant Kirkland was my preaching professor at Princeton Theological Seminary, as well the pastor of numerous churches. I'll never forget a statement he made one day: "Integrity is trumps!"

He's right, of course. The problem is that I'm a flawed human being, unable to live a perfectly integrated life. My sinfulness creates haunting memories of my forgiven-though-not-forgotten past. So, for me, it's good news to hear that God has forgiven me of my sins, accepted me as a beloved child, and adopted me into his family—forever. In light of God's love and grace, I cannot imagine meeting him filled with unforgiveness—particularly in light of Jesus' teaching about forgiveness, which I believe and hold to be true: "When you stand praying, if you hold anything against anyone, forgive him, so that your Father in heaven may forgive you your sins."[5]

The thought of living my life filled with anger and hatred would be enough to fill me with regret. The thought of spending eternity filled with anger and hatred would be a life of endless regret. Inconsolable regret.

Looking for a loophole?

Some people—even Bible-believing Christians—look for loopholes in God's call to forgiveness. After a seminar I conducted at a Bible church, a forty-something woman came up to me, quite upset, and said almost defiantly, "What if the sin Jesus forgave me of is the sin of unforgiveness?"

The situation was awkward to say the least, and I had a number of Bible passages ready to defend myself, if need be. But I had met her before the seminar, and I knew she had recently gone through a very traumatic divorce. What she was really saying was, "Do I have to forgive that no good #@*%! ex-husband of mine?"

I knew, as well, that not every conversation is a teachable moment, and I didn't feel the need to press the point. Being theologically correct seemed less important than being compassionate. At that moment, her personal pain foreclosed her ability to absorb the biblical truths I had presented. The Bible and its teachings will be there for her when, and if, she is ready to revisit the issue.

Like this woman, many of us look for loopholes and excuses to avoid doing what we know we ought to do.

Motivated by religious beliefs

Throughout my years of conducting forgiveness programs, I've learned that a person's faith—including their belief system or attitude—can be, and often is, their source of motivation to forgive. Russie is a good illustration of someone whose Christian faith motivated her to tackle a long-lasting problem in her life. As a Christian, I would say that I have no option but to forgive. Further, I would say that Christianity is impenetrable apart from forgiveness. The cross, symbolic of Jesus' sacrificial death and atoning sacrifice, loses its importance without forgiveness. In unambiguous terms, Jesus says, "If you forgive men when they sin against you, your heavenly Father will also forgive you. But if you do not forgive men their sins, your Father will not forgive your sins."[6] C. S. Lewis, the great author and fervent defender of the Christian faith, put it this way: "To be a Christian means to forgive the inexcusable, because God has forgiven the inexcusable in you."[7]

Echoing this teaching from Jesus, the apostle Paul touches on forgiveness when he reminds us to "bless those who persecute you; bless and do not curse."[8]

Inasmuch as we seek a broad conversation about the topic of forgiveness, and I do not wish to limit it in any way, I will leave an in-depth discussion of other religions for you to explore on your own. I'm simply not qualified to comment with authority on the teachings of religions other than my own, which I have tried to share respectfully, tactfully, and unapologetically.

It is safe to say, however, that all of the world's major religions value the importance of forgiveness, as represented by this excerpt from *The Mahabharata*, an epic poem of Hinduism:

> Forgiveness is virtue; forgiveness is sacrifice. . . . He that knows this is capable of forgiving everything. . . . Forgiveness is truth; . . . forgiveness is holiness; and by forgiveness is it that the universe is held together. Persons that are forgiving attain to the regions obtainable by those that have performed meritorious sacrifices. . . . Forgiveness is the might of the mighty; forgiveness is sacrifice; forgiveness is quiet of mind. Can one like us abandon forgiveness, which is such, and in which are established Brahma, and truth, and wisdom, and the worlds? The man of wisdom should ever forgive, for when he is capable of forgiving everything, he attains to Brahma. The world belongs to those that are forgiving; the other world is also theirs. The forgiving acquire honors here, and a state of blessedness hereafter. Those men that ever conquer their wrath by forgiveness, obtain the higher regions. Therefore has it been said that forgiveness is the highest virtue.[9]

Though I am not a Hindu, I admire their teaching on forgiveness. Further, this poem seems to intersect with Christian doctrine when it says that "persons that are forgiving attain to regions obtainable by those that have performed meritorious sacrifices." The apostle Paul taught that those who habitually harbor hatred will not enter the kingdom of God.[10]

Does a heart full of anger and venomous hatred, whether it is held in our own heart or the heart of our enemies, destroy our communion with God? I saw a bumper sticker once that said, "Heaven is filled with the forgiven, as well as the forgiving." In the end, according to Matthew 6:14–15, they are one and the same: to be forgiving is to find forgiveness, and to find forgiveness is to become forgiving.

Heaven aside, I can affirm without a doubt that people who find themselves trapped in anger, hatred, and unforgiveness experience a living hell on earth. I am committed to helping people experience a little bit of heaven on earth—a life filled with peacefulness, joy, gratitude, and love, the type of life experience described by Piero Ferrucci in his remarkable book *The Power of Kindness*:

> Gone are fear, suspicion, the desire to get even. Forgiving becomes the easiest thing in the world: It is not something we do, but something we *are*. . . . We have only to give ourselves permission to be so.[11]

The Amish have found motivation to forgive, as seen in the aftermath of the deadly school shooting in Nickel Mines, Pennsylvania, in 2006. To be Amish, according to their actions and beliefs, means to be forgiving. Would that all people, including those who call themselves Christian, share in the peace and faithfulness of the Amish.

Some clarifying thoughts on religion

In my role as director of pastoral care, I do not impose my religious beliefs on anyone. Our forgiveness programs at CTCA are all interfaith, and intellectually and spiritually accessible to people of all beliefs systems, including those who claim to have no faith. I can talk for hours about the biological benefits of forgiveness alone, never even raising the topic of religion. However, for those who subscribe to Christianity, I allow Jesus to have the last word on matters of faith, regardless of whether it offends our modern sensibilities.

What motivates people in general, and cancer patients specifically, to want to work on interpersonal forgiveness issues? We know that traumatic experiences often disorient people, and in that state of mind other core issues often come to the fore. For cancer patients, the trauma of facing a potentially life-threatening disease may create the desire to address other aspects of their lives that have come unraveled. Late-stage cancer often triggers long-delayed conversations between family members and friends. Recent research suggests:

> The end of life is a time-intensive crucible in which patients and family members have important things to express to one another. Embedded in this time are two elements of daily functioning: personal relationships and communication. Having conversations about the relationship and communicating love, gratitude, and/or forgiveness may have potential benefits for the dying person and those considered close and important.[12]

I wonder if there isn't a subconscious need to make peace with God, family members from whom they are estranged, and others, in an effort to "tie up loose ends." Surely, this is a motivational force for some people.

Perhaps we do our patients a disservice in avoiding religious teaching, which might address two of the primary barriers to forgiveness: a lack of humility and a disrespect for authority.

Michael McCullough, Kenneth Pargament, and Carl Thoresen have suggested that those who are most likely to be unforgiving lean toward narcissism—people who are egocentric and often have difficulty seeing themselves as the source of other people's pain. What they lack in humility, they make up for in arrogance and self-centeredness. What is often needed to bring humility to a narcissist is a dose of truth—and what could be more humbling than being confronted with the truth that they are living lives inconsistent with what they say they believe?

My interest is not in trying to sell the benefits of having *faith in faith*, but rather trying to help those who have faith reconnect to the source of their faith. Russie and Rich are both Christians, and yet they hadn't allowed their belief system to help them cope with their anger. Faith, as many will attest, can be an incredibly powerful motivator. For those who do not have faith in God, my goal is to love them and to help them heal from the inside out. My faith requires me to heal the sick without judgment or condemnation. If they are Christians, my motivation, in part, is to fulfill the Great Commission, "teaching them to obey all that I [Jesus] have commanded."[13]

A moving target

Motivation, in my life, has been a moving target. What motivated me as a teenager didn't motivate me after I got married and had children. What motivated me then doesn't necessarily motivate me now that I'm an empty nester. What brought a lot of pleasure when I was younger, well . . . not so much now.

The one common thread throughout my life has been goal setting. I've always established and worked toward reasonable, attainable goals. It's unfortunate that some people have to be diagnosed with cancer before they'll make a "bucket list"—you know, a list of things they want to do before they die. One of the lessons I've learned is that there is no guarantee of having a tomorrow. Cancer patients know that full well. Remember Russie's sobering realization: "Whatever I've accomplished up to now might be it." Those of us who don't have cancer need to learn that lesson as well.

Joy and happiness are experienced during the process of accomplishing goals, regardless of how important or insignificant. One day I made it a goal to get my driver's license renewed. It took some time and effort to do it, but after going to the trouble of taking off work early, driving across town, fighting the traffic, and waiting in line at the DMV, the next thing I knew I had a validated license. One more small, but important, task checked off my list—and it felt good.

It may sound trivial, in terms of what I did, but don't miss the point: *Joy is found in setting and meeting attainable goals.* The lesson here is not to wait until you've been diagnosed with cancer to make a bucket list. Make one every day. And if you are burdened with anger and hatred, don't forget to add "forgive my enemy" to your list.

What motivates you?

This chapter was designed to get you to think about the high price of doing nothing about your unforgiveness and to encourage you to think about what it would take to motivate you to forgive. Perhaps your religious beliefs motivate you. Perhaps it's your family and friends encouraging you to fight your cancer, to go toe-to-toe with a painful memory.

Fred Luskin was right. What we need is a book that motivates people to *want* to forgive. As a Christian, the book that best motives me has already been written; which is to say that I count myself among those who hold the Bible to be the Word of God and the ultimate authority in matters of faith and practice.

What or who motivates you?

The Barriers

And it will be said:
"Build up, build up, prepare the road!
Remove the obstacles out of the way of my people."

For this is what the high and lofty One says—
he who lives forever, whose name is holy:
"I live in a high and holy place,
but also with him who is contrite and lowly in spirit,
to revive the spirit of the lowly
and to revive the heart of the contrite."
ISAIAH 57:14–15

Chapter 10

DEBULKING FORGIVENESS

LET'S FACE IT: unforgiveness is a form of cancer that can spread into every part of our lives. It saps our joy, depletes the vitality of our relationships, reduces our quality of life, and can lead to destructive behaviors of all sorts—including the most destructive behavior: suicide. Discussing forgiveness using cancer treatment terms is appropriate, though it may require some definitions and explanations.

In cancer treatment, some cancers are so big and complicated that it's impossible to deal with all of the complexities at once. Because cancers often grow in and around vital organs, their removal requires patience and persistence. In cancer jargon, "debulking cancer" means to make it smaller, usually through radiation, chemotherapy, or a combination of both. Once the tumor has been shrunk, it becomes possible, usually, for surgeons to remove the remaining pieces of cancer. Debulking cancer makes the situation more manageable and increases the likelihood of success.

Healing emotional wounds through forgiveness is similarly complex; so, in this chapter, we'll "debulk" forgiveness so that, in the next chapter, we can identify and remove remaining obstacles.

The biggest pill to swallow: Overcoming self-righteousness

One of the biggest (if not *the* biggest) barriers people must overcome is their feeling of moral superiority or self-righteousness toward the people who caused them harm. Why? Because of our tendency to "demonize" our enemies. We don't want to forgive a demon. We would rather destroy it, and we usually have some pretty good reasons to justify our actions. For example, who could blame Jayne for thinking some pretty bad thoughts about the criminals who had ruined her life? We all get it.

The point is that our enemies are not demons. They're fellow humans. Addressing issues of self-righteousness or moral superiority is an attempt to put a human face on our adversaries, without which it is almost impossible to find forgiveness. Without confronting the completely understandable feeling of self-righteousness, we can often get stuck in a destructive mode and become self-destructive.

Self-righteousness is a strong word, and admitting to it can be a big pill to ask someone to swallow. Remember Jayne's initial response after I suggested that she might need to address issues of self-righteousness? It was a shock to her that I even brought it up. Again, Jayne's response was completely understandable and seemingly justifiable. Unfortunately, it hindered her healing. So, she could hang on to her self-righteous perspective, and everyone around her would understand, but it would keep her from getting to forgiveness.

We all have an innate ability to create distance from our adversaries; and in that distance, we make often well-warranted judgments about them. A criminal is a criminal—but he is also human. Even the worst offender, one who has made an irreversibly huge mistake, is still a human being.

Further, to be human means that we are all victims of other people's meanness, *and*—here's the most important part—we are also *perpetrators of harm*. Let me say it again: To be human means that we are victims *and* perpetrators.

No one escapes the consequences of being human, or the inevitable difficulties created by living with and around other people. We are hurt and we hurt others. As long as we cling to feelings of self-righteousness when we've been victimized, we will never be able to forgive our perpetrators.

Developing a sense of empathy—however small and tenuous—toward the people who have hurt us is a critical bridge to cross. On one side of the bridge stand the self-righteous; on the other side stand imperfect humans with other imperfect humans.

A Hindu proverb

With respect to the creation of empathy, the most powerful metaphor I've found comes from the Hindu *Mahabharata*:

> What can a wicked person do unto him who carries the saber of forgiveness in his hand? Fire falling on the grassless ground is extinguished of itself.[1]

I explain the metaphor this way: Imagine that a meteor falls from the sky and lands in the middle of a tall field of dry wheat. What would happen? There would be an eruption of fire. This is an easy concept to understand. Now imagine that same meteor landing in the middle of a desert, miles from any vegetation. It would hit the ground with a thud, and—apart from the initial impact—there would be no lingering aftershock. No fire. No damage. Only one more rock in the midst of sand and many other rocks.

Now imagine that someone hurls a meteor of sorts at us, a fireball that comes in the form of a harsh word spoken, or a husband who has been kidnapped, or any number of other emotionally traumatic experiences.

If we are a field of wheat, ripe for the harvest: *FIRE!* We will burn with anger, resentment, thoughts of revenge, and our memories of the event will serve as fuel for the flames. But as the proverb reminds us, fire falling on grassless ground extinguishes itself. Is it possible for us to become "grassless ground"? How can we, in light of the traumatic experiences we face, resist becoming ignited with rage, anger, and hatred? And further, assuming that we find ourselves enraged (which is a common human response), how do we put out the fire?

To become grassless ground, more or less impervious to the painful meteors lobbed at us from any number of directions, we must become humble enough to recognize our humanness—that is, that we are both victim and victim*izer*, depending on the circumstances. We both receive and perpetrate harm.

I hurt people, and you do too. We don't always do it intentionally, but our intentions are not the point. Whether we intend to or not, we lob meteors every day that have the potential to hurt someone. In reality, we're all pyromaniacs. The real question is: how are we going to fight the fireballs that are lobbed at us? With fire, or with forgiveness?

In reflecting on his experience with people who were struggling with forgiveness, John Patton writes, "Forgiveness, or something like it, seemed to occur when they are able to see the people who had injured them as different people."[2]

My experience takes that thought a little further: *People are often unable to see other people as different people until they are able to see themselves differently.* Forgiveness can only occur when we see ourselves as different people. As long as we see ourselves as inherently better than other people and beyond the realm of ever having hurt someone deeply, either through our actions or inactions, it is impossible to find the humility required to empathize with the failing of another human being.

According to a study by Julie Exline, "People are more forgiving toward transgressors if they see themselves as capable of committing similar offenses," using such methods as "hypothetical scenarios, actual recalled offenses, individual and group processes, and correlational and experimental designs." Further, "three factors mediated the link between personal capability and forgiveness: seeing the other's offense as less severe, greater empathic understanding, and perceiving oneself as similar to the transgressor."[3]

The Bible teaches that no one escapes sin, and that wrongdoing occurs through both *commission* and *omission*. Sometimes the meanest thing is not what we actually do, but our decision not to offer the help we could have offered. The Bible teaches, "Anyone, then, who knows the good he ought to do and doesn't do it, sins."[4] The truth is, no one escapes this net. Either through what we do intentionally to hurt someone, or through withholding acts of kindness and love, we are forced to admit that, along with everyone else on the planet, we are not perfect. Admitting our own humanity begins the process of becoming "grassless ground."

Children soldiers and Pope Benedict XVI

One of the most humbling truths we face is the realization that, given the right circumstances, we're as prone to violence, evil, and depravity as anyone else. For example, if we had grown up in Sierra Leone, or Somalia, or another culture in which violence is prevalent, chances are we would have gotten caught up in its wake as well. Knowing myself the way I do, it would be pretty arrogant to suggest that I would have avoided participating in violence. I shudder to think of the options that the "child soldiers" face in order to slaughter other human beings. It may be as simple as self-defense: if they don't join in the violence, they will likely become victims of it.

It is widely known that Pope Benedict was a member of the Hitler Youth during World War II, though only briefly and involuntarily. Further, he avoided causing harm to anyone. However, let's not miss the point. In another place or with a little more time, his life might have been forced to take a different path. If I had lived in Nazi Germany as a youth, I probably would have been in the Hitler Youth as well. Even more sobering is the fact that German clergy, with a few exceptions, notoriously cooperated with the Third Reich.

If I had been born into a culture of kidnapping, torture, and mayhem, who knows what I might have been capable of doing in the name of survival? It is humbling to think of how fortunate I am to have grown up where I did, and how tragic it is for the young people who find themselves engaged in horrific acts that they—under different circumstances—might have avoided.

Remember Jayne's experience? She reached the point of asking herself, "How can I forgive these horrible people?" Eventually, she began to imagine them as children and what their lives must have been like in order for them to grow up to become such brutal human beings.

Although Jayne's experience was horrific, and her personal life was literally invaded by thugs bent on destroying anything and anyone in their path, it represents a relatively small percentage of human tragedy. The more common kind of forgiveness issues tend to be less extreme: divorces, betrayals, emotional abuse, mean-spirited words spoken in the heat of an argument, cruel but not illegal behavior—in short, the kind of things that we are all potentially capable of, should the circumstances present themselves.

Though we may not have been child soldiers, we mustn't be so naïve as to think the potential to have been one doesn't lie hidden in our DNA, lurking in the murky waters of our subconscious mind, with one primary goal: survival.

Motivation to forgive can be forged on the anvil of personal survival. People can become motivated to overcome hatred because of health and religious benefits, and it's a good start. Along the way, though, our memories will bring us face-to-face with our perpetrators; and unless we can find some sense of empathy for them, progress often stops.

Trust me, you will never want to forgive a demon. Instead, you will seek out ways to destroy them, at least subconsciously, and you will feel justified in doing so.

The challenge is to put a human face on those who have hurt us. It's possible to forgive a flawed human being, because down deep we know, as Jayne came to realize, we are flawed as well.

American culture

Even though America is not Sierra Leone, there are still cultural forces that shape us and too often form barriers to motivation.

Forgiveness takes effort. It takes time, energy, and intentionality. Forgiveness and its benefits, therefore, must be something we highly value. If our values are determined by how we spend our resources, such as time, money, and talent, a good case could be made that American culture creates and often celebrates a culture of violence. We are probably too close to the forest to see the trees, so to speak, but many Americans simply do not understand who we really are and what we have become.

We need look no further than the media response to the Amish schoolhouse shootings I mentioned earlier. Reporters seemed somewhat surprised, even shocked, by the Amish response to the tragedy. Why? Is it because forgiveness has become countercultural? Is it the rare exception rather than the rule?

How wonderful it would be if instead we were shocked by an attitude of vengeance. But we aren't stunned by vengeance. It seems to be the norm, and the proliferation of lawsuits is probably as good an indicator as any. We really do want our pound of flesh.

Our cult heroes are too often rappers promoting violence, or movies and TV shows whose displays of violence numb the conscience as well as the soul. We are no longer appalled and disgusted by actions born of hatred; rather, we are becoming the mean and malicious people we should otherwise abhor. The air we breathe is not the celestial air of forgiveness but rather the toxic air of hatred. Unlike the peace-loving Amish, the mean and malicious mainstream don't want to forgive and forget. We want—and believe we deserve—something quite different: an eye for an eye and a tooth for a tooth. All without counting the cost to our collective soul.

I am not the first to mourn the coarsening of the American soul. Others much brighter than I have trumpeted the concern, yet perhaps none more eloquently than Robert F. Kennedy:

> Some look for scapegoats, others look for conspiracies, but this much is clear: violence breeds violence, repression brings retaliation, and only a cleansing of our whole society can remove this sickness from our soul. . . . Our lives

on this planet are too short and the work to be done too
great to let this spirit flourish any longer in our land. Of
course we cannot vanquish it with a program, nor with a
resolution.[5]

Kennedy was, by any measure, a dreamer and an idealist. But I
share the dream of a land known not only for its military might and
strength but also for its ability to ascend to the moral high ground,
able to forgive our enemies while at the same time protecting and
defending ourselves from harm.

"Of course we cannot vanquish it with a program, nor with a
resolution," Kennedy said. It is naïve to think that hatred will be
vanquished, but the reshaping of our culture is possible with forgiveness as its cornerstone. Just ask Nelson Mandela.

Canadian culture

We Americans are not alone. A Canadian blogger recently
lamented the lack of forgiveness in his own culture:

> I have been thinking about forgiveness over the last little
> while. . . . Basically, it boils down to the fact that there is no
> longer any room to make mistakes. There's no tolerance for
> uncertainty. . . .
>   I think we see it most in our political culture. We don't
> give politicians an inch. If a mistake is made, we pounce
> on it. We demand to know what went wrong, we ask for
> a resignation, or—in typical Canadian fashion—we call
> for an inquiry. We demand explicit promises and we won't
> tolerate a shift in planning when the facts on the ground
> change.[6]

We do seem to live in a culture that is "ready to pounce." Maybe
that's the down payment for increased secularization of our society.
Having said that, let's not excuse our faith communities for their
part in the secularization process. The truth is that Christians have

often been poor witnesses to the good news they claim to believe. Christians, including myself, can be as unforgiving as any nonbeliever. Everyone has room to improve in this area, especially if the dream is to create a "culture of forgiveness."

Cancer and hatred: The two biggest plagues we face

I would argue that, despite what Robert Kennedy said, perhaps there *is* a resolution and a program worth considering: a resolution to create a more forgiving country, and a public education system that requires forgiveness education as part of its curriculum. Who could be against that? After all, the two biggest plagues we face are cancer and hatred—and perhaps, in a very real way, they are related.

If not in our schools, then certainly we should teach forgiveness in our churches, synagogues, mosques, meeting houses, and other places of worship. After all, doesn't every religion value forgiveness? I'm not so naïve as to think that forgiveness is the solution to all of the world's problems; but without knowing how to forgive someone who has hurt us, we will default to our base instincts of anger, hatred, violence, and revenge. The clear air of forgiveness awaits all who truly yearn to breathe free.

One contemporary scholar, Charles Griswold, suggests that "forgiveness (unlike apology) is inappropriate in politics" and that only in certain circumstances is "forgiveness an appropriate response to the wrongs that plague human life in every valley of our troubled earth."[7] Though in his book he intentionally excludes the healing of emotional wounds, opting for a more philosophical discussion of the topic of forgiveness, it serves as an important reminder that, at the highest levels of scholarship, religious or secular, theological or medical, academic or clinical, forgiveness is a topic that is discussed philosophically. As a case in point, a friend of mine recently completed a course on forgiveness at Princeton Theological Seminary, at the end of which he didn't have the faintest idea how to help someone learn how to forgive. Instead, he said, the class approached the topic of forgiveness from a theoretical point of view. Such is the status of discussion in this country, and perhaps elsewhere.

On the other hand, South African Archbishop Desmond Tutu overstates the case when he says, "Without forgiveness, there is no future."[8] Clearly, the archbishop meant that without forgiveness, there is no *future worth living into.* My patients, suffering with cancer, are not the least bit interested in the philosophy of forgiveness. Sometimes not even religion. Nevertheless, those who desire a future, however measured, intuitively sense truth and wisdom in Tutu's profoundly simple statement: *Without forgiveness, there is no future.* Life gets very real when you are diagnosed with stage-IV brain cancer, feeling as if you are buried under a collapsed Haitian building, wondering, "Is there anyone who can help me?" Avoidance is a problem, to be sure. But the problem is exponentially compounded when our leading lights are not asking the right questions, thereby creating a null curriculum, an absence of answers to the questions that, at the ground level, matter most.

Time heals all wounds, right?

In the next chapter, we'll discuss in more detail the role of time in the process of forgiveness, but because our thoughts and belief systems often affect our motivation, a few words on the subject here seem warranted.

It is an absolute truth that "insight [won't] work with people who are unmotivated to change." If, for example, someone doesn't want to learn, it doesn't matter how brilliant the teacher is. And even the dullest people can learn if they have enough drive. Human beings can always find a reservoir of strength and determination, somewhere deep inside, if they are truly willing to seek it.

However, when it comes to forgiveness, success may not be a function of sheer willpower. It may simply be that the injury wasn't sufficiently painful to prompt the person to deal with it. He or she might choose instead to let time heal the wounds—which it can't and won't.

What often happens when we try to let time heal our wounds is that we adjust to our painful situation by creating a "new normal," or new emotional baseline. The effect of this emotional adjustment and accommodation is that we begin to think of our new emotional state as good and normal. *For many people, it has been so long since they have been happy that they don't remember what it feels like.* When you ask them how they're doing, they immediately say, "Fine!" But ask them how they are really doing, and they often respond with tears.

Daniel Gilbert, in his profoundly insightful book, *Stumbling on Happiness*, makes the following observation:

> When experiences make us feel sufficiently unhappy, the psychological immune system cooks facts and shifts blame in order to offer us a more positive view. But it doesn't do this *every* time we feel the slightest tingle of sadness, jealousy, anger, or frustration. Failed marriages and lost jobs are the kinds of large-scale assaults on our happiness that trigger our psychological defenses, but these defenses are not triggered by broken pencils, stubbed toes, or slow elevators. Broken pencils may be annoying, but they do not pose a grave threat to our psychological well-being and hence do not trigger our psychological defenses. The paradoxical consequence of this fact is that it is sometimes more difficult to achieve a positive view of a *bad* experience than of a *very bad* experience.[9]

Perhaps some people don't concern themselves with forgiving medium-grade offenses because they just aren't painful enough. If that is the case, it certainly makes sense. But, unfortunately, many people believe that time will heal even the most severe emotional wounds.

In either event, here's the problem: *time doesn't heal wounds.* Instead, it simply gives us an opportunity to adjust, reframe, shift, and adapt our emotional landscape, with the unfortunate result that even moderately annoying memories can potentially become toxic ones.

We also cannot assume that people will deal with their most painful memories, either. Our research actually suggests otherwise. What we think we have learned is that there is a shortage of clergy, psychologists, and psychotherapists who are equipped to help people learn how to forgive.

Discussions of forgiveness occur much less frequently than they should. The helping professions do not have the tools required to meet the need; the emotional demand far exceeds the supply of schooled healers. On top of that, I have yet to find a seminary, university, or medical school that teaches its students to help people learn how to forgive. Furthermore, "How to Forgive" is not a course that is offered in the School of Life.

When religion is an obstacle

One more note about religion, which, you'll notice, also made my list of possible motivators in the previous chapter. Though it can be one of the most powerful motivational tools at our disposal, religion occasionally stands in the way of forgiveness.

Although I don't apologize for my faith, I want to make clear that, for some people, the Bible can be an impediment to forgiveness. The rigid dogmatism—in any religion—can create shame in some people who may perceive themselves as being unworthy or unfaithful. They are guilt-ridden because of their inability to forgive—or to even find forgiveness desirable. Against the backdrop of severe trauma, some people may even perceive forgiveness as something repugnant.

I am aware that my voice may not be heard by some who have suffered emotional trauma. I only hope and pray that someday—and I hope sooner than later—they will be able to begin the process. If you are one of those people, here's what I would say: If Jayne, Russie, Cathy, Rich, and Sharon were able to forgive, I hope that you will find a way to forgive as well. Of this I am sure: A "feeling of lightness" is possible for you.

Some clinical researchers, even those claiming a Christian heritage, are tempted to back away from some of Jesus' teachings. Perhaps they're concerned about doing more harm than good by invoking some of his undeniably rigid statements. For example, in the parable of the unmerciful servant in Matthew 18, the unforgiving servant is thrown into prison until he can repay his debt, because of his unwillingness to forgive a small debt owed to him after having been forgiven an enormous debt. The Greek translation is even more startling; it says that he is given to the "torturers to be tortured."

The message behind the parable is this: People who are unforgiving can expect to feel tortured. We can imagine the legitimate response from a rape victim: *Tortured [by God] for being unforgiving! Are you kidding me?*

These words fall hard on severely wounded people. Expecting a rape victim to forgive the rapist seems only to add insult to injury. Her feelings are, at one level, completely understandable. On the other hand, Jesus—who himself suffered insult *and* injury—should be allowed to have the last word when it comes to matters of forgiveness, and he says we're to forgive "seventy-seven times."[10]

It may not seem fair—right now. It may not make sense—right now. It may create anger at God—right now. But all I can say is this: Many people, including some who have suffered enormously, have found the ability to forgive those who caused them harm. One day, when you are ready, you may be able to forgive as well. Until then, think of Eva Mozes Kor, who as an Auschwitz survivor found the ability to forgive Dr. Mengele and others. I am happy to give Eva the last word in this book, and I invite you to read the epilogue and reflect on her life, much of which is, for most of us, unimaginable.

Chapter 11

RELEASE!
The Healing Power of Forgiveness

Surely you desire truth in the inner parts;
you teach me wisdom in the inmost place.
PSALM 51:6

Nanotechnology

Cancer treatment, happily, has advanced through the new use of nanotechnology, which is the science of dealing with particles and dimensions at the atomic level. Instead of traditional surgery, nanotechnology is a noninvasive technique that allows doctors, in certain circumstances, to excise primary tumors that otherwise would be considered inoperable.

Wouldn't it be nice if our emotional wounds could be healed as easily? Forgiveness education attempts to heal emotional wounds that compromise abundant living; and though we haven't yet advanced to the use of nanotechnology, we now have a better under-standing and appreciation of the impact of forgiveness at the cellular level. This increased understanding didn't just happen, however.

Like nanotechnology, it is the result of exhaustive research, study, reading, reflection, experimentation, exploration, and trial and error.

In this chapter, we will address some additional obstacles to forgiveness, and I will outline a technique—called *narrative therapy*—that has proved helpful to my patients. I'll also explain *why* this technique may help you in finding forgiveness. Narrative therapy crystallizes the results of my lengthy research, study, and experimentation, and I offer it with the hope that it will help others benefit from and build on what I have learned about the important topic of forgiveness.

Further, it captures the essence of the forgiveness education program we've developed at Cancer Treatment Centers of America, known as: *Release! The Healing Power of Forgiveness*. This chapter fills in some of the remaining gaps, closes some loopholes, and gives a quick overview of what I think is both *minimally* and *critically* important to know about the process of forgiveness.

Myths about forgiveness

A *myth* can be defined as "a popular belief or tradition that has grown up around something or someone," or "an unfounded or false notion."[1] Numerous myths, or false notions, have grown up around the topic of forgiveness. Here are some of the most common:

Myth: Forgiveness = Reconciliation

In short, forgiveness involves only one person: *you*. Reconciliation involves two or more people. To *reconcile* means "to reestablish a close relationship between," or "to settle or resolve."[2]

As you may recall, understanding the difference between forgiveness and reconciliation was one of Russie's "aha!" moments. She said, "It was very freeing, because I had this idea that if we forgive someone then we have to socialize with them; we have to be with them all the time and we have to say, 'What you did was okay.'" Who knows how Russie came to believe this, but it is an all too common misconception.

To be reconciled means to reestablish harmony with someone, to work through the problems between you. Marriages are reconciled when couples jointly address their problems. Coworkers can work through their issues and be reconciled as well. But as the old saying goes, "It takes two to tango." So, you can forgive someone who has been dead for thirty years—but you will never be reconciled to that person. Forgiveness requires only one person: *you*.

There is no relationship between forgiveness and reconciliation, except to say that when two people find reconciliation, they've probably also found forgiveness. Reconciliation often follows forgiveness, but not always. Russie's reestablished relationships with her boss and uncle attest to the possibility of reconciliation, as does Cathy's reconciliation with her ex-husband. But forgiveness is no guarantee of reconciliation.

It is more than unlikely that Jayne will ever be reconciled to Eduardo's kidnappers. But she was able to forgive them. A divorced couple can find forgiveness, but renewed harmony, or true reconciliation, is very uncommon. For that matter, some people are so toxic and dangerous (physically and emotionally) that it doesn't make sense to even be around them. To the extent we have control in the situation, people who are continually callous, mean, and emotionally toxic forfeit our presence. It doesn't mean we hate them. It doesn't mean we haven't forgiven them. It doesn't mean we can't wish them well. It doesn't mean we desire evil to befall them. It simply means that we have the right to choose not to be physically or emotionally connected to people who treat us poorly. Forgiving someone from the heart does not require that we check our brains at the door and create another opportunity for injury. We can wish the person well—from a distance.

Yet it is very common for people, even well-seasoned clergy, to believe that forgiveness is synonymous with reconciliation. Reconciliation is wonderful, often desirable, and in the best of circumstances, might even be advisable, but it isn't the same thing as forgiveness.

The Bible encourages reconciliation. For example, Jesus taught: "If you are offering your gift at the altar and there remember that your brother has something against you, leave your gift there in front of the altar. First go and be reconciled to your brother; then come and offer your gift."[3] However, *both parties must desire to be reconciled.* Jesus' teaching presumes that your brother isn't going to attack you when you seek reconciliation. Certainly, during the process of reconciliation, you must be careful not to place yourself in harm's way.

The difference between forgiveness and reconciliation can be condensed into this thought: You can forgive someone without being reconciled, but reconciliation usually includes forgiveness. You can let go of the anger and forgive without having to see, or spend time with, the other person again.

I'm sure you would agree that it's a good thing that our emotional health and wellness does not ultimately depend on the willingness or availability of someone else to be reconciled.

Myth: Forgiveness = Forgoing Justice

God is a God of mercy and forgiveness, but he is also a God of justice. Mercy and justice are not mutually exclusive; they go hand in hand, as Jesus reminds: "Woe to you, teachers of the law and Pharisees, you hypocrites! You give a tenth of your spices—mint, dill and cummin. But you have neglected the more important matters of the law—justice, mercy and faithfulness. You should have practiced the latter, without neglecting the former."[4]

- Forgiveness does not negate the consequences of breaking the law.
- Forgiveness does not mean letting people off the hook.
- Forgiveness does not mean there are no consequences for someone's behavior.

Let's say that you are hit by a drunk driver on your way home. You are badly injured and your car is totaled. Is it possible to forgive the person who hit you? Yes, absolutely. But that doesn't mean he or she won't be arrested for DUI, together with whatever other consequences there might be, including a forfeited driver's license, financial responsibility for the damages, and more. From your hospital room, you can wish the other driver well, in addition to cooperating with the authorities as they enforce the law; but under no circumstances should you ever take the law into our own hands.

According to the Bible, God has instituted social order through governmental laws and ordinances. Justice, it is expected, will be mediated through these God-ordained institutions. Noteworthy is the apostle Paul's admonition in the book of Romans: "Do not take revenge, my friends, but leave room for God's wrath, for it is written: 'It is mine to avenge; I will repay,' says the Lord."[5]

Paul elaborates on this in the following chapter of Romans:

> Everyone must submit himself to the governing authorities, for there is no authority except that which God has established. The authorities that exist have been established by God. Consequently, he who rebels against the authority is rebelling against what God has instituted, and those who do so will bring judgment on themselves.[6]

To be sure, we must "let justice roll on like a river,"[7] but not through personal vendetta or by playing judge, jury, and executioner. Jayne and Eduardo, for example, should allow the Mexican government, as imperfect as it may be, to capture, prosecute, convict, and sentence the kidnappers—though I'm sure it might be satisfying, and perhaps understandable, to consider other scenarios.

There is a high price for doing nothing. There may be an even higher price for doing the wrong thing in pursuit of justice.

Myth: Forgiveness = Mental Consent

Forgiveness does not come from simply saying, "I forgive you." It requires a heartfelt change through which the anger and hatred are transformed into feelings of peaceful indifference or neutrality. Here's an illustration:

Several years ago, a twenty-five-year-old woman came to my office to speak to me. As we settled into the conversation, she began pouring her heart out about the horrible relationship she'd had with her father. Seven years earlier, she had gotten into a quarrel with her father in front of a group of friends. A tussle ensued, during which her sweatshirt came off, and she was humiliated by the indecent exposure (for obvious reasons). In her anger and shame, she had left home and hadn't seen her father since, even to the point of homelessness, sleeping in her car.

Often in pastoral conversations, there isn't much dialogue. The time is spent simply "holding a bucket" for people: just listening as they vent their anger and frustrations. Understanding that, I listened for nearly half an hour as she tearfully unburdened herself by reliving her memories of her father. After twenty-five minutes, I asked her this question: Have you ever thought of forgiving your father? She immediately responded by saying, "Oh, I forgave him a long time ago!"

Had she forgiven her father? Obviously not. She was as angry with him that day in my office as she had been when she left home seven years earlier. However, like most professing Christians, she knew the "right answer" was forgiveness, and so she said, "Oh, I forgave him a long time ago!" But forgiveness is not merely "speaking the right words."

Some might argue that there are two kinds of forgiveness: *decisional* and *emotional*. Decisional forgiveness equates to mere mental consent, which I would argue is sub-Christian in that Jesus requires forgiveness from the heart.[8]

Beyond theological differences, decisional forgiveness seems to push back against most secular research on the subject, which supports the idea that forgiveness is a process that begins with *a decision to forgive* and ends with *a change of heart toward the perpetrator.*

Further, "empirical research has shown that this [i.e., "decisional forgiveness"] approach is marginally effective in improving a client's stress levels or emotional health."[9]

In 2006, *World* magazine columnist Andrée Seu wrote an article on forgiveness titled "The Thing We Don't Do." Though Seu is not involved in forgiveness research, she intuitively realizes that forgiveness requires more than "mental consent":

> Forgiving is the hardest thing you will ever do. That's why most people don't do it. We talk about it, cheer for it, preach on it, and are sure we've practiced it. But mostly the illusion of having forgiven is that the passage of time dulls memory. The ruse will come to light with hair-trigger vengeance when fresh offense hurls in to empty out the gunnysack of half-digested grievances. I asked a few people if they'd ever forgiven anyone, and what it felt like. They gave me answers so pious I knew they'd never done it.[10]

Forgiveness is not merely speaking the words. Instead, an emotional shift must take place in the forgiver. Jayne, Sharon, and others describe it as "a feeling of lightness." Russie described it as "a cheer in my heart that wasn't there before." Just speaking the words "I forgive you" will neither lighten nor cheer your heart.

Revenge feels good

Schadenfreude is satisfaction or pleasure felt at someone else's misfortune. The term derives from the German words *schaden*, meaning "adversity" or "harm," and *freude*, meaning "joy." I recently experienced schadenfreude at my wife's expense. Kay and I rented a lovely house that had a few drawbacks—such as lizards running around the backyard, and occasionally in the house. Knowing my wife's fear of creepy-crawly things, I bent down and tickled the bottom of her leg—which caused her to shriek and me to howl! I was laughing so hard, I didn't even notice that she was beating my arm black and blue (and deservedly so). Causing her to "suffer" in this way gave me great joy. In fact, just thinking about it makes me laugh. Thinking about doing it again makes me smile! No doubt, the suffering she inflicted on me made her feel a little better too.

We all have moments when we feel satisfaction or pleasure at someone else's misfortune. Revenge, or thinking about revenge, plotting revenge, or thinking about past experiences of revenge—all of these trigger similar responses. Revenge is schadenfreude, but with a more sinister overtone.

An article in *Psychology Today* captured a secular view of revenge, with a touch of schadenfreude:

> Revenge is like a prescription medication: A little can cure you, a lot can kill you, and you should avoid getting hooked. It is best if you can do without it, but if you must have a dose, the best approach is: Get even, get over it, and get on with your life.[11]

It's hard to believe that any credible therapist would encourage anyone, even halfheartedly, to "get even." *Psychology Today* is a credible magazine representing many points of view, therapeutic styles, and techniques . . . but "get even"?

Having said that, I understand the human need to feel vindicated, as I've had my own fair share of stabs in the back, so to speak. In the face of being on the receiving end of human meanness, what seems to be a more appropriate response and obvious source of relief than an act of vengeance? Even something as simple and innocuous as honking your horn at someone who unexpectedly cuts you off—it seems like the right thing to do, *and it makes you feel good!* Schadenfreude!

Recent research helps us better understand the biology of revenge; that is, why it makes us feel good. Revenge is sweet, researchers have learned, because acts of revenge stimulate the same part of the brain that produces endorphins, which mimic morphine. A new brain-imaging study suggests that we feel satisfaction when we punish others for bad behavior. In fact, anticipation of this pleasure drives us to crack the whip, according to scientists behind the new research.[12] In other words, we seem to be biologically hardwired to seek revenge; it's in our DNA.

If that is true, why is it wrong to think such thoughts?

After years of contemplating this curious reality, I've come to this conclusion: If God had not given us an innate desire for revenge, we would have no desire to right wrongs. Seeking justice would evaporate into indifference. If someone hurt us and we didn't have a feeling of vindictiveness or revenge, we would likely shrug our shoulders and say, "Whatever." But we ought not to shrug off hurt or injustice, as if they don't matter. Justice is important, and the biological impulse for revenge is the trigger *to begin the process* for seeking and obtaining justice. Nevertheless, it is one thing to have the process begin, it is another to get stuck with chronic feelings of anger and revenge. To the extent that feelings of revenge activate the process of justice seeking, it is helpful. To the extent that feelings of revenge cause us to take the law into our own hands, or do nothing at all, it is harmful—to ourselves and others.

Justice is more than simply getting even. It requires utilizing available resources, such as telling the teacher, calling the police, or filing a formal complaint with human resources. It might be as simple as confronting people with their wrongdoing, because they might be unaware of the offense.

Further, as I mentioned earlier, one of the great life lessons I have learned is that my enemies are not always wrong. I may feel very strongly about a situation and be completely wrong. Likewise, revenge may make us feel good, but we may find out we didn't have our facts straight and so we become part of the problem instead of part of the solution.

Jayne wanted to lop off the heads of her husband's kidnappers like a Samurai warrior. Who could blame her? Revenge, even *contemplating* revenge, makes us feel good, but it is a far cry from justice. Jayne and Eduardo's need for revenge, for righting their horrible wrong, has manifested itself in seeking justice through media interviews and high-level discussions with government officials in both Mexico and the United States.

Forgiveness and prayer

John Calvin, more than 450 years ago, wrote, "The rule we should observe whenever we are either upset by fear or oppressed with grief is to raise our hearts to God at once. There is nothing worse or more harmful than inwardly brooding over what torments us."[13] Calvin observed the negative effects of inwardly brooding over things that bother us. His solution? Prayer. Not because Jesus taught his disciples to pray, though that was always in the background for Calvin. He offered prayer as a faithful way to cope with both our adversity as well as our adversaries. Prayer makes us feel better about both.

Jesus said, "But I tell you: Love your enemies and pray for those who persecute you."[14] Though most of us know that we should pray for our enemies, how many of us actually do? To borrow Andrée Seu's comment about forgiveness, praying for our enemies is probably "the thing we don't do." As a pastor and theologian, I know we should pray for our enemies; but I am also a researcher trying to help people understand the "biology of faith." As such, I occasionally find research that catches my eye, including this result from a recent study: "A single prayer for a loved one led to increased self-reported willingness to be forgiving of that person."[15]

I believe this to be true and can explain the psycho-spiritual processes that allow it to happen. My explanation will also serve as a framework for better understanding other helpful activities that we recommend to our patients during their search for forgiveness.

When we pray for someone, what are we doing? By the very nature of prayer, we intentionally and unavoidably focus our hearts and minds on two things—the person who harmed us and the situation that created the harm—and place them both before God. As we pray for our enemies, we deliberately resist the temptation to either avoid or ignore the person or the situation. And, according to the study, as we do this, we find ourselves more open to *want* to forgive the perpetrator. Contemplating the person and revisiting the situation set the stage for healing. Presumably, the more frequently we pray, the better we are likely to feel . . . over time.

MODERN MEDICINE MEETS ANCIENT WISDOM

People of faith have experienced the benefits of prayer from the beginning of time. None of this should surprise us. God does not engage in schadenfreude; he does not delight in torturing us— although, admittedly, praying for our enemies is almost torture for some of us. God wants us to find healing, and healing comes from the process of revisiting old emotional wounds through prayer.

Time does not heal old wounds

Modern medicine has discovered the ancient path of healing that prayer has offered to people of faith for centuries. Through a newly discovered "somatically based therapy" for post-traumatic stress disorder (PTSD), treatment now includes the following elements:

- Establishing a safe and secure place for the patient.
- Finding the subtle body sensations that are linked to the trauma.
- Eliciting these sensations in the environment of perceived safety.
- Identifying sensations are brought out slowly in order to avoid overwhelming the patient, which is called *flooding*.
- To avoid flooding, the patient is subtly transitioned back and forth between the "safe place" and the painful memory or perception.[16]

The Veteran's Administration (VA) has fortunately found great success using this type of therapy in treating soldiers who have been traumatized by their experiences in Iraq and Afghanistan.

To again underscore the importance of healing old wounds, Robert Scaer, MD, reminds us that "until the trauma victim physically completes the successful resolution of the traumatic experience, he continues to demonstrate behavior that is stereo-typed, repetitive, and counterproductive to ongoing daily life experiences. He responds to new events, relations, and challenges as though he were responding to an old threat."[17] Time does not heal old wounds.

Instead, according to Scaer, the old wounds may worsen with the passage of time, almost as if they had a life of their own.[18] This process is known as *kindling*. It is as if people are living in the past, and are destined to allow the past to constantly intrude on their daily lives. Without help, their future is their past.

My relationship with my father attests to the phenomenon of kindling. My father was not physically or emotionally abusive; although he had some rough times in his life, he didn't take his frustrations out on me. My anger toward my father grew out of his absence in my life. He was physically absent because he worked evenings; and when he was home, he often isolated himself in his bedroom.

Though it didn't bother me much growing up, once I left home it began to bother me a lot because of a growing awareness of how important fathers can (and should) be in the lives of their children. Further, my father died when I was in my twenties, foreclosing the opportunity for further involvement with me. I was angry at him in my twenties, but by the time I was in my late thirties, the anger had grown into full-blown hatred. Through counseling, I was able to reach the point where I could forgive my father—after he had been dead for fifteen years.

The truth I encountered while struggling to forgive my father was that I hadn't been the perfect son, either. In the midst of tears (I was thirty-nine years old, for heaven's sake, and he had been gone for a decade and a half!), I asked my father (in my mind) to forgive me for being an imperfect son. That was the truth that set me free and my moment of "lightness." Forgiving my father was almost secondary. For fifteen years, I had avoided facing my anger at him, and over time it had gotten much worse. Kindling. Time hadn't healed the wound, after all.

Virtual Iraq: Facing our demons

Following the general guidelines listed above, the VA's somatically based treatment for PTSD requires traumatized soldiers to revisit their battlefield experiences within the safety of a warehouse in the US. The trauma could have been caused by any number of battlefield events: IED explosions, Humvee attacks, being shot at, experiencing the death of another soldier, and other similar situations. Obviously, these memories are horrific and often debilitating. One key to successful treatment of PTSD is having the soldiers intentionally commit themselves to addressing their emotional pain instead of avoiding it.

Dr. Michael Kramer, a clinical psychologist at the VA hospital in Manhattan says, "One of the hallmarks of PTSD is avoidance. Patients spend an awful lot of time and energy trying not to think about it or talk about it. But behaviorally, avoidance is what keeps the trauma alive. With virtual reality, we can put them back in the moment. And we can do it in a gradual, controlled way."[19] In another *New York Times* article about PTSD therapy, James Dao reports:

> Therapists at several military and veterans hospitals are also using a system known as Virtual Iraq to treat posttraumatic stress disorder. The system, based on a computer game called Full Spectrum Warrior, helps patients to reimagine, with the help of virtual reality goggles and headphones, the sights and sounds of combat experiences as a way of grappling with trauma.[20]

In other words, through a technique commonly referred to as *exposure therapy*, traumatized soldiers find healing for their emotional wounds, not by *avoiding* their mental and emotional situation but by *intentionally revisiting* the battlefield through reimagining the traumatizing event. As they are exposed to the hurtful events over short periods of time, the pain is lessened and their fears are relieved. Under the supervision of trained colleagues, traumatized war veterans have been able to face their demons, and in facing them, find the ability to overcome the debilitating effects of PTSD and find the healing they deserve.

Narrative therapy

The psycho-neurological pathway that veterans travel through exposure therapy is the same pathway traveled by those who engage another helpful technique commonly referred to as *narrative therapy*. In an earlier chapter, I mentioned the wonderfully helpful work done by James Pennebaker, PhD. Here's what some of his seminal research has disclosed:

- Scholars suggest that "a personal coping style that suppresses negative emotion may increase the risk of cancer."[21]
- "Trauma writing has been associated with biological markers of enhanced immune functioning"[22]
- "Writing and/or talking about emotional topics has also been found to influence immune function in beneficial ways, including t-helper cell growth."[23]

At this point, we shouldn't be surprised at these findings. We've well established that suppression of negative emotions depletes the body's ability to defend itself from disease. Finding creative ways to revisit emotional wounds and express the pent-up feelings in a safe environment contribute to the healing of those wounds. Prayer offers this. Exposure therapy offers this, as does narrative therapy. Following Pennebaker's lead, we have our patients at CTCA engage in writing exercises. We ask them to write about their traumas as follows:

1. Write in the safety of their home, hotel, or hospital room.
2. Write three times for twenty minutes each within a twenty-four- to thirty-six-hour period.
3. Be sensitive, during the writing, to irrational thoughts or judgments made about the people who harmed them. Often

what keeps us trapped in anger are irrational thoughts or untruths we tell ourselves. We believe the truth will set our patients free from their pain if they honestly seek it.

4. Writing is nondirected. We do not tell people what to write about, though we do share that writing in letter form has proved helpful.

5. We ask that they write about the same situation or experience each time. If there are multiple forgiveness issues or various perpetrators, we ask them to focus on just one situation at a time.

6. We ask that the letter not be sent to the perpetrator.

7. We never ask to read the letter. In fact, we encourage them to wad it up and throw it away if they would like to do so. These are private, personal moments and are often accompanied with tears.

8. We ask them to pray during the process.

It is during these prayerful writing exercises that our patients usually find their release, their feeling of lightness and peace. Forgiveness in their hearts. But, again, it isn't simply the writing that brings relief; it is the desire for healing that causes the patients to pick up their pens and write in the first place. If their hearts are not fully committed to finding healing through forgiveness— or they are not committed to seek the complete truth about their situation—they could write for years and never find the relief they are seeking.

Here's what I want you to learn: *narrative therapy is not a psychological gimmick*. It is a process in which the actual writing plays only a small part. Equally important is the education that takes place before the writing, including the spiritual component: removing myths, addressing ego-related issues, and framing the process of forgiveness in a way that allows the person to enter into it without fear or unrealistic expectations.

Whether the method is through prayer, narrative therapy, or exposure therapy, or a combination of all three, the pathway is a similar one. Healing found through any of these methods is a miracle from God.

Modern medicine's helpful therapeutic techniques are often not so new after all. Healing is available through prayer, as well as through other helpful techniques. We mustn't avoid our demons—we must face them and forgive them. But as long as we want to destroy our demons, we will never find the ability to forgive. Putting a human face on those who have harmed us is critical. Through prayer and other helpful techniques, we find that our anger is lessened and our desire to destroy is reduced. It is when we put down our spears that we find God doing something new in our lives.

The Waorani

Over a period of several generations, the Waorani tribe of Ecuador became one of the most violent cultures ever documented. Blood-feuding and revenge killing reduced the numbers of the group dramatically, almost to the point of extinction. Up to 60 percent of deaths among the Waorani were due to murder.[24] However, beginning in the mid-1950s, the Waoranis' narrow, violent culture was changed into a peaceful one in an evolutionary nanosecond. How? Through forgiveness.

In 1956, a group of five American missionaries, led by Jim Elliot and pilot Nate Saint, made contact with the Waorani in the Ecuadoran jungle. Two days after a seemingly friendly contact with three Waorani villagers, the five missionaries were speared to death by a larger group from the same clan.

In response to these killings, however, the law of retribution, *lex talionis*, was set aside and replaced with an even greater law: the law of love. Evil was not returned for evil. The cycle of violence did not continue. For the first time, the Waorani learned another way of living: a life not bent on revenge and hatred, but one of love and forgiveness. Over time, the Waorani came to attribute this peaceful, forgiving lifestyle to the missionaries' religion and the God they worshipped. Eventually, many converted to Christianity. One Waorani warrior remembered the experience with these words:

Before the missionaries came and taught us about God, we lived spearing. Back and forth, back and forth we speared, they died. After hearing and believing in God, we ceased killing others back and forth. Forgiveness led to religious conversions, which led to more forgiveness which led to more conversions.[25]

The point here is not to establish Christianity as a superior religion, but rather to open conversation about how forgiveness, displayed so self-sacrificially by the Christian missionaries, might help transform our own society, beginning with our homes, schools, churches, synagogues, and mosques.

The apostle Paul offers a catalog of behaviors that, if habitually embraced, bar entrance into the kingdom of heaven. Among them are "hatred, discord . . . fits of rage."[26]

If that is true (and I believe it is), the realization of heaven on earth may be possible if we truly allow God's Spirit to guide us away from hatred, and into love, through forgiveness.

Chapter 12

SELF-FORGIVENESS OR SELF-ACCEPTANCE?

Why in the world did I do that?
ST. AUGUSTINE

SOME PEOPLE WILL likely skip to this chapter without first reading the other eleven. Why? For several reasons, the most obvious of which is that it seems harder to forgive ourselves than it is to forgive others; anything that can shed light on this difficulty offers everyone the possibility of relief. A less obvious, though very important, explanation is that self-forgiveness highlights our flaws and foibles, which we tend to focus on. That's why we have a tendency to

  rubberneck at traffic accidents,
  glance at sexy pictures or revealing attire,
  focus on the most unattractive personality characteristic in
    others, as well as in ourselves,
  stare at roadkill,
  peek disapprovingly at ourselves in the mirror,
  blame others for our mistakes,

look before we flush,
rehash unpleasant memories, *especially* our own, and
rationalize our behavior.

There is no level of spirituality that allows us to transcend basic human instincts for more than a short period of time. No one is immune to the impulses demanded by our DNA. And though, with God's help, we can learn to manage our weaknesses and satisfy our hungers rightly, we will experience moments of weakness and failure. After we do these things—these sometimes silly, occasionally sick, stupid, self-gagging, self-disappointing things—we are haunted by the question: *Why in the world did I do that?* Often, we're afraid of the answer, so we dismiss the question instead of wrestling with it.

Alan Jacobs, in his very satisfying book *Original Sin: A Cultural History*, reminds us that even the great theologian St. Augustine of Hippo struggled with this basic question:

> In one of the most famous passages of his *Confessions* he describes a sin of his childhood, the theft of pears from a neighbor's orchard, and the tone of the whole passage is befuddlement: *Why in the world did I do that?* This became a recurrent theme for him as he reflected on his life.[1]

It is a recurrent theme for most of us. The truth is, there is something about us that makes us want to sniff around our decomposing, decaying memories. And the more horrific the scene of our accident, the more we tend to linger and wonder: *Why in the world did I do that?* The answer is that we are living, breathing contradictions. We are paradoxes, often self-contradictory—a thought captured well in this Puritan prayer:

> O Changeless God,
>   Under the conviction of thy Spirit I learn that the more
> I do, the worse I am, the more I know, the less I know, the

more holiness I have, the more sinful I am, the more I love, the more there is to love.

O wretched man that I am! O Lord, I have a wild heart, and cannot stand before thee. How little I love thy truth and ways! I neglect prayer by thinking I have prayed enough.

My mind is a bucket without a bottom, with no spiritual understanding, ever learning but never reaching the truth, always at the gospel-well but never holding water.

My conscience is without conviction or contrition, with nothing to repent of. My will is without power of decision or resolution. My heart is without affection, and full of leaks. My memory has no retention, so I forget easily the lessons learned, and the truths seep away.

Give me a broken heart that yet carries home the water of grace.[2]

Indeed, this prayer displays the complexity of the human heart. We are capable of great love and goodness, while at the same time fickle and seemingly unable to fully control our thoughts and behaviors. *Why in the world did I do that?* Because that is what it means to be human: a living, breathing enigma.

As the story is told, *The Times* of London once sent out an inquiry to famous authors, asking the question, "What's wrong with the world today?" G. K. Chesterton, author and Christian apologist, responded simply and with astonishing honesty:

Dear Sir,
I am.
Yours,
G. K. Chesterton.[3]

Perhaps the sincerest followers of Jesus, in the end, are the ones who live without pretension of perfection, but rather maintain a keen—though uncomfortable—acceptance of how unlike God they truly are. Consider this parable told by Jesus:

To some who were confident of their own righteousness and looked down on everybody else, Jesus told this parable: "Two men went up to the temple to pray, one a Pharisee and the other a tax collector. The Pharisee stood up and prayed about himself: 'God, I thank you that I am not like other men—robbers, evildoers, adulterers—or even like this tax collector. I fast twice a week and give a tenth of all I get.' But the tax collector stood at a distance. He would not even look up to heaven, but beat his breast and said, 'God, have mercy on me, a sinner.' I tell you that this man, rather than the other, went home justified before God. For everyone who exalts himself will be humbled, and he who humbles himself will be exalted."[4]

The parable of the Pharisee and tax collector suggests that the one who found favor with God wasn't the overtly pious Pharisee, but the humble, contrite tax collector, who, aware of his sinfulness, begged God for mercy.

Don't look back long

Hugh White, a nineteenth century U.S. Senator from Tennessee, once said, "When you make a mistake, don't look back at it long. Take the reason of the thing into your mind and then look forward. Mistakes are lessons of wisdom. The past cannot be changed. The future is yet in your power."[5]

Unfortunately, it seems that some of the things we've done are so ugly and smelly—and therefore so compellingly attractive—that regardless of how repugnant, spiritually damaging, or physically harmful it is to chew on the cud of past sinful indiscretions, we seem to want to at least *check it out*. We sometimes find ourselves getting addicted to the scent. Why? Because "the scent" confirms what we have always suspected about ourselves: Regardless of our public persona, we know that, *at our core*, we are an enigmatic, inconsistent mess.

Self-forgiveness provides, yet again, an opportunity to gaze at our self-inflicted wounds, whether they are real or perceived, and ask ourselves for the umpteenth time, "Why in the world did I do that?" Perhaps that is why many people will skip to this chapter, without having read the previous ones.

Cancer patients, physicians, and caregivers

Psychological research suggests there is a huge need for self-forgiveness. For example, many patients diagnosed with breast cancer think they could have prevented their disease if they had been sufficiently proactive in their self-care. One study concluded that "women who blamed themselves reported more mood disturbance and poorer quality of life than those who did not blame themselves. Analyses revealed that self-blame for cancer partially mediated the relationships between a self-forgiving attitude and both mood disturbance and quality of life."[6]

One recent research project concluded the following:

> A self-forgiving attitude and spirituality may benefit breast cancer survivors who blame themselves for their cancer. One hundred and eight women with early breast cancers completed questionnaires assessing self-blame, self-forgiveness, spirituality, mood and quality of life (QoL) in an outpatient breast clinic. Women who blamed themselves reported more mood disturbance and poorer QoL. Women who were more self-forgiving and more spiritual reported less mood disturbance and better QoL. Interventions that reduce self-blame and facilitate self-forgiveness and spirituality could promote better adjustment to breast cancer.[7]

A recent visit with a group of cancer patients made me very aware that it is not only breast cancer patients who struggle with self-forgiveness. All of the patients told me that they continually wonder what they could have done to prevent their disease and usually find something they could have done differently; thus they live with feelings of self-condemnation.

A case study

Here's a generic story that serves as a paradigm for many untold stories:

Once upon a time, CM did something he was terribly ashamed of doing. The pain continued for years. Not a day went by that CM didn't kick himself for making such a stupid mistake. It was as if he were literally lying on the ground, kicking himself over and over for a past blunder.

One day, something snapped, and CM had a moment of personal enlightenment. It didn't come from anything he had read, studied, or taught. Rather, it followed from asking himself, *How long are you going to continue to kick yourself? Get up! You are not perfect. Nobody is. Stop being so hard on yourself.* So CM, wearied by self-judgment, forgave himself and chose to stop the kicking. Suddenly, he felt better and wiser.

He tired of his continual self-berating attitude and decided that the time had come to let it go. Like Forrest Gump, who, after months of mindlessly running back and forth across the country, suddenly stopped in the middle of the California desert. When his followers asked him why, Forrest said: "Because I'm tired. I think I'll go home now." So CM decided it was time for him to forgive himself for his misdeed.

So far, so good. Who among us can't identify with this man? We've all done things that we wish we hadn't done, borne the pain of self-loathing for a time, and then decided to move on. My guess is that few readers would, on the face of it, ridicule CM for wanting to find personal peace.

What if?

But what if the "mistake" that he was "terribly ashamed of doing" was child molestation? This hypothetical case study raises a number of important questions:

- Should the weariness of his burden be self-mitigated? Should he be encouraged to alleviate his pain?
- Morally, should CM have the right to relieve himself of the seriousness of his behavior?
- At what point, if any, in the continuum of morality is it appropriate to forgive oneself?
- Further, if this book were made available to inmates on death row, is the lesson I want them to learn simply, "Look, I know you are in pain, but really, you ought to forgive yourself"?
- Do the ripple effects of CM's behavior on the life of the child he molested and the child's family suddenly become so inconsequential that we are now rooting for CM to "find personal peace"?

I'm not suggesting that CM cannot find forgiveness from God, or even from the molested child; but is self-forgiveness the solution we want to offer him? Do we really want to encourage this man to let himself off the hook as if he is the only one who matters? Or is this behavior and misdeed one that should never be forgotten, a burden he must forever bear and for which he should always accept some sense of personal responsibility, even though it might always be uncomfortable and inconvenient?

The ethical dilemma

The ethical dilemma created by this story is this: Should the desire for emotional well-being be the only determining factor in whether or not self-forgiveness is the appropriate cure for internal suffering? Is a person's emotional weariness a sufficient standard for seeking self-forgiveness? Or, do we live in a culture that believes that personal discomfort is so abhorrent that a remedy, however easy or difficult, must be offered to ease the pain?

There are at least three obvious remedies for the personal pain and torment associated with wrongdoing:

1. Do nothing, which will continue the pain.
2. Forgive yourself, which, in theory, frees you from your painful past.
3. Accept yourself, which includes dealing with reality by accepting responsibility for your actions and creating a cascade of healthier possibilities, such as repentance, restitution, etc.

Self-blame and self-forgiveness

Research supports the idea that people often blame themselves for their diseases. At its most basic level of understanding, self-blame translates into thinking negative thoughts about ourselves. The antidote often offered by therapists is *self-forgiveness*. However, forgiveness presumes wrongdoing. Forgiveness presumes that there was something the person did—or didn't do—to cause the disease or undesirable situation. What if a situation arose in which there was nothing a person knowingly could have done or should have done differently, but he or she still suffers from a disease or other malady?

It is important to remember that our subconscious minds cannot distinguish between a real or perceived threat. Regardless of whether we could have prevented a situation or disease, to the extent we think we could have prevented it, our bodies will respond accordingly, creating a cascade of negative emotions and biological responses. If a problem is real to the patient, it's a real problem. This is true even outside the realm of disease.

For example, let's say two grandparents allow their grandson to ride their four-wheel ATV on their farm as long as he wears a helmet and rides safely. Before too long, however, the young man crashes the ATV, causing horrific brain injuries and multiple other traumas. The grandparents had done their due diligence by reminding him to wear his helmet and ride safely, but they are nonetheless devastated by the outcome of the accident.

In this illustration, I am trying to create a scenario of complete innocence (the opposite of CM's situation) in which, on the face of it, the crash was simply an unavoidable accident, the kind that happens every day. We cannot predict everything that is going to happen to us; we cannot take every precaution possible. Apart from being overly neurotic, no one lives life that way.

Some natural questions arise from this scenario:

- Should the grandparents feel self-blame?
- If they did nothing wrong and this was just an unpreventable accident, would inviting them to forgive themselves be good, healthy, appropriate advice?
- Would it be helpful to them?
- Might it be harmful?

Self-forgiveness presumes wrongdoing. If there is no wrongdoing, there is no need for forgiveness. To borrow from attorney Johnny Cochran: *If the glove doesn't fit, you must acquit.* In our example, self-forgiveness is a completely inappropriate remedy, because it requires the grandparents to accept responsibility for something that was out of their control, something for which they are blameless.

I suspect it doesn't matter how innocent the grandparents were or what advice we give to them—they are going to feel deep, deep pain for the rest of their lives, simply because that is the nature of the human heart. Furthermore, the only people who will find relief in offering self-forgiveness as a solution to their pain will be the well-meaning friends and counselors who offer the advice. The grandparents will likely take their pain and guilt to the grave.

Similarly, physicians often suffer when a prescribed treatment fails, even after their best efforts.[8] Caregivers suffer from issues related to self-forgiveness because they often feel as if they didn't do enough to help their loved ones.[9]

I know a man who lives in self-condemnation because he allowed his son to buy and drive a motorcycle—with fatal consequences. Smokers who get lung cancer often suffer similar self-loathing.

I have my own list of things I wish I hadn't done. You do too. No one would argue that the need to feel unburdened from past mistakes is enormous, but is self-forgiveness the best advice we have to offer? Or is it simply the easiest?

Is there such a thing as self-forgiveness?

As we've already seen, self-forgiveness is complicated and confusing. Experts in the field of forgiveness, such as Michael McCullough, refer to self-forgiveness as "a confusing concept." Everett Worthington has written about the inherent problem of self-forgiveness: "To forgive myself, I am in two roles at the same time. I am the victim. I realize that my sinful act damaged me at the core of my being. But, I am also the transgressor; I did the sinful act. That dual role makes self-forgiveness complicated."[10]

Further, Paul Vitz and Jennifer Meade convincingly argue that self-forgiveness cannot be done with any degree of objectivity. In the end, we cannot be both judge and jury and trust that the verdict rendered is anything more than an attempt to find relief from haunting memories through an experience of "cheap forgiveness."

> These negative feelings can be experiences of loneliness, sadness, depression, self-hate, and condemnation, and they are the major clinical expressions resulting in self-forgiveness therapy. These are very real types of suffering and rightly cry out for an answer. It is the contention here, however, that such painful feelings persist because of reasons other than a failure to forgive the self.[11]

Rightly calling out for an answer

Throughout history, people have tried to find ways to cope with self-condemnation and guilt. Sacrifices to the gods were offered by the Greeks, Romans, Babylonians, Hittites, Egyptians, and Jews. In antiquity, the Jews would offer an *olah* (meaning "what goes up"), a burnt animal or grain offering, as expiation for their sin, which served not only as an atonement or reparation for whatever they had done but was also the mechanism God used to help his people relieve their guilt and shame. Christians find their atonement with God mediated through the sacrificial death of Jesus on the cross.

The point here is that, throughout history, all people everywhere have struggled with the psychological and emotional burden created by wrongdoing, real or perceived. People of all times and in all places have been crying out for an answer.

Enlightenment

The Greek word for "enlightened" is *photizo*, stemming from the root word *phos*, which means "light." *Photizo* is defined as follows:

1. to give light, to shine
2. to enlighten, light up, illumine
3. to bring to light, render evident
   a) to cause something to exist and thus come to light and become clear to all
4. to enlighten, spiritually, imbue with saving knowledge
   a) to instruct, to inform, teach
   b) to give understanding to.[12]

To be *en-lighten-ed* means to find knowledge and spiritual insight; it means to be illuminated. And though the process of forgiveness (whether self-forgiveness or interpersonal forgiveness) involves each of these, the Bible rejects the idea that humans can enlighten themselves. For example, from the Old Testament we read:

> For You will light my lamp;
> The LORD my God will enlighten my darkness.[13]

And from the New Testament:

> It is impossible for those who have once been enlightened, who have tasted the heavenly gift, who have shared in the Holy Spirit, who have tasted the goodness of the word of

God and the powers of the coming age, if they fall away, to be brought back to repentance.[14]

According to the Bible, God is the author of all good things, including enlightenment. Inspiration, knowledge, and most importantly, wisdom are gifts from God, as is alluded to in the book of Proverbs:

> For the LORD gives wisdom,
> and from his mouth come
> knowledge and understanding.[15]

We can argue over which religion is the most enlightened. We can debate the superiority of one philosophy over another, dissect the strengths and weaknesses of arguments, and parse one another's words and their meanings, but we can't get away from the fact that we are corrupted and corruptible beings in need of something more than self-forgiveness. In the Bible, when King David tries to cover up his adultery with Bathsheba by sending her husband, Uriah, to his death in battle, God doesn't tell David to forgive himself "because 'everyone makes mistakes.'"[16] And Jesus, as he hung dying on the cross, did not look upon those gathered and say, "Forgive yourselves. You don't know what you are doing."[17]

Self-forgiveness is not a biblical concept

Although the Bible acknowledges the existential need to seek and find emotional and spiritual relief created by the burden of sin, it doesn't provide a recipe for self-forgiveness. It simply isn't there. Then again, the Bible doesn't mention or explain many other important topics as well. For example, the Bible doesn't offer answers to these important questions:

1. Where did God come from?
2. If God created humanity for his pleasure, why did he allow us the ability to make mistakes that cause his displeasure?

3. Is the world God created the best of all possible worlds?
4. Why would God allow poverty, hunger, human meanness, and evil to be interwoven into the reality of our everyday existence?

These questions, as important as they are to us, are completely ignored.

The list of questions that the Bible *doesn't* answer—at least not to any degree of satisfaction—is a long one. Unfortunately, those questions include these two:

> *Can I forgive myself?*
> *If so, should I?*

Regardless of whether you view the Bible as the inspired Word of God or merely as a repository of more than four thousand years of wisdom literature, there is no dictate, teaching, or command to forgive yourself to be found in its pages.

Forgiveness, according to the Bible, is only from God toward his people—and then, because we were created in God's image, from his people to one another. One could argue that God was unwilling to allow his creatures to dismiss or delete their past mistakes as if they had never happened and to simply free themselves from the pain and guilt of the past.

Self-forgiveness, it seems, is dismissed out of hand in the Bible. We are given remedies for pain, but those remedies do not include self-forgiveness.

The ripple effects of our behavior: Unknowable consequences

Furthermore, it is impossible to appreciate the implications and impact of our mistakes. As the Bible reminds us, the sins of the fathers are visited upon the children to the third and fourth generation.[18] Who am I to forgive *myself*, knowing that the ripple effects of my behavior will likely affect the lives of my children and grandchildren?

For example, if a father is a thief and his children follow in his footsteps, he may, at some point, feel bad when he learns that one of them has been arrested for stealing. He may even regret having been a horrible role model and—in theory—forgive himself for being such a bad example. Okay so far. But how will he feel the next time they steal? And the time after that? And the time after that? Perhaps the better question is this: How *should* he feel? Should he feel responsible? ashamed? indifferent?

Or, similarly, a father directly or indirectly teaches his son that making money and accumulating wealth is what life is all about. So the son becomes obsessed with materialism, only to learn that the more money he makes, the more spiritually and emotionally bankrupt he becomes. Money does not bring happiness after all. The father bears witness to his son's decay and regrets that he never taught him that there was more to life than a large financial portfolio. The father forgives himself for being an imperfect father after the son's first trip to rehab. How should he feel after the second relapse? Callously indifferent? responsible? ashamed?

The point is this: What does self-forgiveness accomplish? In these situations I've suggested, self-forgiveness seems capricious and self-indulgent, even if it does bring moments of fleeting emotional relief. Ethically, self-forgiveness seems inappropriate, even though the burden is understandably difficult.

In light of this reality, what does self-forgiveness promise? One thing it can never do is stop the ripple effects of our behavior. Our sins will continue to affect the lives of others in unknowable ways and with unforeseen consequences.

Recent research

Regarding the concept of self-forgiveness, Paul Vitz and Jennifer Meade make the following observations:

- Prior to recent decades in the United States, self-forgiveness appears absent from all psychological literature.
- Although the distinctive concept of interpersonal

forgiveness has deep and ancient roots in Judaism and Christianity, nowhere in those long traditions are adherents instructed to forgive themselves. Rather, the opposite is true: only God or the person who has been sinned against can forgive wrongdoing.

- Self-forgiveness is a very recent concept, with only modest psychological validation, and very little or no theological justification.
- It is not surprising that self-forgiveness theories have developed in the present cultural period with its strong emphasis on the autonomous and narcissistic individual.[19]

Is it possible that the concept of self-forgiveness is simply the result of godless people seeking godless answers? Is it an expression of our innate ability to rationalize our behavior, regardless of consequences, reframing our actions so that our egos don't collapse under the weight of our shame? Is it the logical continuation of the self-help ethos, which, in encouraging people to follow their bliss, tries to find a way through the inevitable pain to a more emotionally satisfying state?

Perhaps, but it is not that simple. As Vitz and Meade point out, the most common advocates of self-forgiveness are "religious psychologists."[20] I confess to occasionally slipping into these discussions, because at times self-forgiveness seems like a quick solution to needless suffering.

But here's the problem: After I give my sage advice, I am probably the only one who feels better. For those who realize the implications of their behavior, for those who understand that they are "not an island, but part of the main," self-forgiveness almost never works. Their conscience won't allow them to feel indifferent.

First base is usually reached on our knees

To the extent that narcissism is an impediment to forgiveness, then its antidote is humility. Michael McCullough, Kenneth Pargament, and Carl Thoresen define humility as follows:

To be humble is not to have a low opinion of oneself; it is to have an opinion of oneself that is no better or worse than the opinion one holds of others. It is the ability to keep one's talents and accomplishments in perspective. To have a sense of self-acceptance, an understanding of one's imperfections, and to be free from arrogance and low self-esteem. Humility has been tied to a number of health outcomes, in that a lack of humility is a risk factor for coronary heart disease. It is not surprising, then, that humility should play such a vital role in the process of forgiveness. To forgive, one must have the capacity to identify with others and view them as more than simply extensions of oneself. One must be able to feel a modicum of social interest, a willingness to admit a personal role in relationship dysfunctions, and genuine concern and empathy for others to be motivated for reconciliation.[21]

The better and safer net

Regardless of whether the issue is interpersonal forgiveness or self-forgiveness, the better and safer net to jump into is *self-acceptance*. Why? Because we can't change the past.

What's done is done, and merely forgiving ourselves in order to feel better creates little or no likelihood that our lives will change. The psycho-neurological pathway toward relief that is offered to a wounded soul shouldn't detour around personal accountability. Self-forgiveness promises a detour and a shortcut, an easy way out. It may, however, lead us back to where we began—to the reality of what we have done.

Even for a cold-blooded killer, self-acceptance requires facing reality, which can lead to the possibility of new life. The apostle Paul, before his conversion, had Christians arrested to be killed and was an onlooker at the stoning of Stephen, the first Christian martyr.[22] King David had Uriah the Hittite killed to cover up a sin. If there was hope for these two, then there's hope for us all.

Self-acceptance offers a legitimate and healthy way to healing: the best road to travel out of a painful past.

I agree with Paul Vitz and Jennifer Meade that "self-acceptance" better describes the emotional and spiritual processes that are often described as "self-forgiveness." I can learn more and more to accept myself as a flawed person. I can accept that my flaws will affect my life and the lives of others, including people I know best and love most. I can accept responsibility for my actions and seek to right the wrongs I have created. But forgive myself? Just shrug off my misdeeds as if nothing happened? I hope not. One researcher described self-forgivers with these words:

> The portrait of the self-forgiver . . . is a person who is narcissistic, self-centered, and overly confident, as well as devoid of appropriate shame or guilt. However, if the person is not narcissistic to begin with, he or she is apparently likely to become more so through the self-forgiveness process.[23]

The Bible presumes, from the very beginning, that the human condition is utterly and absolutely imperfect. From the get-go, we are all flawed. Adam ate the apple. Abraham lied to Pharaoh about his wife's identity and allowed her to be taken into his harem without so much as a "Hey, wait a minute!" The patriarchs were all flawed, including King David, who was nevertheless called "a man after God's own heart."[24]

The beauty of the biblical witness is that it refuses to make the human condition appear less depraved or more humane than it really is. The Bible doesn't turn Abraham into an airbrushed version of a perfect man. He is seen as flawed, though with great faith.

The lives of all of the great biblical characters, both men and woman in the Old and New Testaments, are shamelessly transparent and exposed. Why? Because they were what we are: a *mess*. We're flawed. We make mistakes.

According to a biographer of C. S. Lewis, the great Christian author and apologist loved to skinny-dip. Thomas Merton, by all accounts one the most influential Roman Catholic writers of the mid to late twentieth century, experienced a brief, torrid affair with Margie Smith—in addition to other unseemly behavior. Singer/songwriter Joan Baez, who befriended Merton, once said of him: "Watching him drinking and in love showed me how the greats are human, too."[25]

I'm not offering excuses, or legitimizing anyone's behavior. I'm not suggesting that we learn to tolerate inappropriate, immoral, or unethical behavior by anyone, clergy or otherwise. What I'm asking for is a reality check.

The fact is, we screw up in the most unbelievable ways. And there has never been a single moment in recorded history when it was ever any different. Making mistakes is an unfortunate but undeniable part of our DNA. If self-forgiveness were a command, we would spend all day, every day, engaged in an effort similar to trying to rub off the color of our skin—and with equal results.

Life as it is

Any recipe for self-acceptance should include the following ingredient: self-acceptance of our humanity *as it is*, not how we might hope *it would have ideally been* in another life and time. This thought is masterfully penned in the lesser-known second half of Reinhold Niebuhr's *Serenity Prayer*:

God, give us grace to
accept with serenity the things that cannot be changed;
Courage to change the things which should be changed;
and the Wisdom to distinguish the one from the other.

Living one day at a time;
Enjoying one moment at a time;
Accepting hardship as a pathway to peace;
Taking, as Jesus did,
This sinful world as it is,

Not as I would have it.
Trusting that You will make all things right,
If I surrender to Your will,
So that I may be reasonably happy in this life
And supremely happy with You forever in the next.
Amen.[26]

One barrier faced by most adherents to organized religions, including Christianity, is that outsiders consider them hypocritical. Sadly, when we are accused of being hypocrites, few of us know how to respond to the accusation. At a deeper level, we might even agree with our accuser because we know our own hearts, and we do not live up to our own expectations, much less anyone else's. But are we hypocrites?

As R. C. Sproul cogently reminds us, hypocrites are those who say one thing and do another. Christians are not hypocrites, because we don't make the claim that we are perfect.[27] Quite the contrary. We admit we are messed up in every way, from sun up to sun down, but that God loves us in spite of our flaws and failures. The same way he loved King David, Abraham, Adam, and all the other flawed patriarchs and heroes of the faith. The good news (the *gospel*) is that we are loved by God, in spite of our sinfulness.

We must accept the world, including our part in it, *as it is, not as we would have it.*

What should I do with this pain I feel?

If, as I and others propose, the goal isn't to forgive ourselves, as modern psychology suggests, then what? What should we do with our pain?

After an innocent tragedy . . .

After being diagnosed with an unpreventable disease . . .

After I make mistakes and do dumb things . . .

After I ask myself, "Why in the world did I do that?" What should I do with this pain I feel?

Viktor Frankl, the well-known Holocaust survivor and esteemed psychotherapist, often began his counseling sessions with the question, "Why do you not commit suicide?" From there, it is said, he found the basis for his psychotherapy, a style he called *logotherapy.* His goal was to "weave these slender threads of a broken life into a firm pattern of meaning and responsibility."[28] The challenge for every counselor or therapist is to help "awaken in a patient the feeling that he is responsible to life for something, however grim his circumstances may be."[29]

Whether we are innocent survivors of the Holocaust or perpetrators of wrongdoing, the solution Frankl holds out to sufferers is the same: Resist the understandable temptation to forgive ourselves, and instead ask ourselves, *What does life (God) demand of us?*

In light of our mistakes, God expects something from you and me—and it isn't self-forgiveness. It isn't letting us off the hook through blaming, rationalization, or forgiving ourselves. It isn't spiraling into self-punishing masochistic behavior. It isn't looking for an easy way to rid ourselves of pain or escape from our circumstances.

The consequence of engaging in wrongdoing is not that we find a way to rid ourselves of the pain through self-forgiveness. In my view, to encourage my patients to self-forgive would create more anxiety for them, because I would be asking them to do something that either can't be done (as with the grandparents in my earlier example), or helps to foster narcissistic tendencies (as with the child molester CM). At some point, our lives need to be about *we* and not *me.*

Rather, we should ask ourselves this question: In light of my grim situation, what does God require of me? The Bible teaches that God requires the following responses (for starters):

- that we accept 100 percent responsibility for our behavior;[30]
- that we repent, turn to God, and prove our repentance through our good deeds;[31]
- that we are truthful with ourselves because the truth will set us free;[32]
- that we confess;[33]

- that we forgive others;[34]
- that we act justly, love mercy, and walk humbly with God;[35]
- that we accept that some painful memories are "thorns" that will not be removed.

The apostle Paul writes:

> There was given me a thorn in my flesh, a messenger of Satan, to torment me. Three times I pleaded with the Lord to take it away from me. But he said to me, "My grace is sufficient for you, for my power is made perfect in weakness." Therefore I will boast all the more gladly about my weaknesses, so that Christ's power may rest on me. That is why, for Christ's sake, I delight in weaknesses, in insults, in hardships, in persecutions, in difficulties. For when I am weak, then I am strong.[36]

The point here is that some thorns, regardless of how they got there, will not be removed by God or anyone else. They are a God-given "hair shirt" that serves as a reminder that God both cares and disciplines.

We can complain about the thorns in our sides, or we can accept them. We can be miserable, or we can find purpose, meaning, and even joy in the midst of our suffering and pain. The thorns are there for a reason, with a purpose that may be readily obvious or a purpose that will remain a mystery. They may actually be survival cues that serve as a warning to a long-past threat. For some people, the only thing worse than remembering a wrongdoing is repeating it. The thorn, in this case, serves as a reminder, and should be welcomed instead of resisted.

Be kind to yourself.

Learn the lessons, gain the wisdom, bear lightly the memories, and move on, even if it's with a limp.

Remember that you are one of the most important people in your life. Like the rest of us, you are not perfect.

The Bible does not offer self-forgiveness as a solution to our mistakes. It offers saving grace given from an understanding, compassionate God to people who have come to *accept themselves* for who they truly are, not who they pretend to be; for who they are, not who they had hoped to become.

Power made perfect in weakness? When I am weak, then I am strong? This is what God demands of me, and I believe he demands the same of you: strength through weakness. Another paradox.

How grim are your circumstances? In light of them, what does God demand of you?

CONCLUSION
Cool Quickly

YOU REMEMBER FROM an earlier chapter the proverb, "Fire falling on grassless ground is extinguished of itself." This teaching points to the possibility that when—not if—people hurl their fiery, mean, hurtful comments and actions at us, we will not explode in kind through flaming rage, anger, and hatred *if* our hearts are "grassless ground."

With God's help, we can cultivate hearts that are grassless ground, so when we find ourselves hurt by others, or even by self-inflicted wounds, we will cool quickly. Like Jesus. Like Nelson Mandela. Like the Amish. Like Jayne, Russie, Cathy, Rich, and Sharon. Like the Waorani warriors who learned from the example of others: Do not spear.

Not surprisingly, the people we seem to need to forgive the most are the people we are around the most often. Spouses. Coworkers. Children. Neighbors. Because familiarity breeds contempt, we are often the most unforgiving of the people we know the best—they seem to jab or spear us the most frequently. In little ways (and sometimes in big ways) people are just plain irritating. I often tell my patients that it is easier to forgive someone who has been dead for thirty years than someone you sleep with every night. How are we to relate to these occasionally difficult people? How do we cope with the daily irritations created by simply being around them?

By becoming grassless ground. We need to cultivate a heart of forgiveness that expects people to act like people, even if it means betrayal by a familiar friend. King David shares a similar disappointment, when he writes:

> Even my close friend, whom I trusted,
> he who shared my bread,
> has lifted up his heel against me.[1]

Why should we be surprised or irritated when someone honks their horn at us the minute the light turns green? Or when someone blurts out something hurtful and mean? I used to get steamed, but now I laugh and say, "Uh oh. Someone is unhappy."

A forgiving heart does not return evil for evil; instead, it understands that the human condition is so flawed that doing inappropriate and hurtful things is what flawed people inevitably do.

We wonder, *Why in the world did they do that?* But we mustn't forget that we also wonder the same thing about ourselves.

Forgive those who persecute you. Seek justice if they have harmed you (or others). But expect to be disappointed by people—including those you know best and love most. Bless them, do not curse them.

A heart that is grassless ground:

Expects people to disturb your peace;

Expects people to act selfishly;

Expects people to do or say hurtful things;

Expects people to, on occasion, try to take away things you care about very much, such as your good name and reputation, or even someone as special as a parent, child, spouse, or friend.

My colleague Charlotte Witvliet learned about forgiveness following the tragic loss of her father in a preventable car accident. The other driver who caused the accident? She forgave him.

Ev Worthington, a leading researcher in the field of forgiveness education, came home one day to find his mother brutally murdered. The murderer? Ev forgave him.

The Amish in Nickel Mines, Pennsylvania, forgave the murderer of the innocent little children in the schoolhouse. How were they able to so readily offer forgiveness? They had cultivated it throughout their lives so that when grassless ground was required, it was there in abundance.

My enemies? Forgiven.

And yours? Forgive them and wish them well.

Prepare your heart daily. Pray for your enemies. Pray for those who persecute you. Pray for yourself, even as you anticipate your own daily transgressions.

And when grassless ground is required of you, may there be found a fruitful harvest of love and forgiveness. May there be an acceptance of life and people as they are, not as you would have them be.

EPILOGUE
Eva's Story

Surviving the Angel of Death
By Margo O'Hara[1]

Eva Mozes Kor and her twin sister, Miriam, survived the Holocaust and the Auschwitz concentration camp, where about 70,000[2] people died during World War II. The girls were ten years old when they entered the camp, and spent nine months there before it was liberated. Twins, including Eva and her sister, were subject to cruel experiments, procedures and injections under the direction of Dr. Josef Mengele, also known as the Angel of Death.

. . . . [Eva] overcame her pain by forgiving those responsible for the Holocaust, including Dr. Mengele. She recently wrote a book for young adults, *Surviving the Angel of Death*, and previously was the subject of the documentary, *Forgiving Dr. Mengele*. . . .

What is your message about forgiveness?

The interesting thing about forgiveness is [that] it's not about the perpetrator. Victims [who don't forgive] are always asking who did what to me. "If I could only find all the pieces . . ."

Living under that mind-set is a tragedy. Sixty-five years later, I've gotten power to myself and freed myself because I deserve to be free. The perpetrators might not, but I do.

It's a mental trap that people fall into. They get more and more involved and under the thumb of the perpetrator. Then voluntarily you are remaining the victim.

Did your sister feel that way?

No. She died before I stumbled upon that idea of forgiveness.

How did you stumble upon that idea?

I was curious to know why this Dr. Munch would meet with me.[3] I was blown away with the respect he showed me. I asked him about the gas chamber and he explained to me how it worked. I got a Nazi to acknowledge the gas chambers and so I asked him to go back to Auschwitz with me and sign a document that acknowledged the gas chambers. This wasn't a survivor saying it, this wasn't a liberator saying it. It was a Nazi.

So I wanted to thank him for what he had done. Does anyone know how to thank a Nazi? My number one lesson is to never give up. And for ten months I asked myself, "How do I thank a Nazi doctor?"

What I discovered about myself was an amazing thing. What I discovered was I, a little nobody, had the power of forgiveness. I had the power to forgive. No one could give me that power. No one could take it away.

So I wrote a letter of forgiveness and I knew Dr. Munch would like that.

What do you think would have happened if
you hadn't met Dr. Munch?

That's the million-dollar question. I don't know what would have happened.

What is the next step after forgiveness?

The world is filled with people filled with pain. Real or perceived, it doesn't matter. If we teach our kids how to forgive, we could raise a world that is much, much happier.

What is the thing that is most misunderstood about forgiveness?

Forgiveness has the reputation that the perpetrator has to be sorry. The biggest misconception is that [forgiveness] is for the perpetrator. It's strictly a gift of freedom I give myself. It's free! You don't need an HMO. There are no side effects, and it works. It's like a miracle drug.

Instead of changing the world—that's too big of a job—we have to repair it one place at a time. . . .

Jayne forgave her husband's kidnappers.
Russie forgave her uncle.
Cathy forgave her ex-husband.
Rich forgave a boss.
Sharon forgave her mother.
Eva forgave Dr. Mengele and Dr. Munch.

These are signs of hope for us all. May God bless you in your journey for health, happiness, and peace with God. And if it's a miracle you need in order to forgive someone, trust me, they happen every day whether you believe in them or not.

NOTES

Introduction • Cancer and Hatred

1. Carl E. Thoresen, Alex H. S. Harris, and Frederic Luskin, "Forgiveness and Health: An Unanswered Question," in *Forgiveness: Theory, Research, and Practice*, ed. Michael McCullough, Kenneth I. Pargament, and Carl E. Thoresen (New York: Guilford, 2000), 269.
2. Nathaniel G. Wade and Everett L. Worthington Jr., "In Search of a Common Core: A Content Analysis of Interventions to Promote Forgiveness," *Psychotherapy: Theory, Research, Practice, Training* 42, no. 2 (2005): 160–77.
3. ThinkExist Quotations, http://thinkexist.com/best_friend _quotes/ (accessed May 15, 2010).
4. Richard L. Stanger, "Václav Havel: Heir to a Spiritual Legacy," *Christian Century*, April 11, 1990, 368–70, http://www.religion -online.org/showarticle.asp?title=767.
5. David Prescott, "The Christian Church: Engaging the Future," 2001, http://www.religion-online.org/showarticle.asp ?title=2295.

Chapter 1 • Cooling the Fire Within

1. National Cancer Institute, "Executive Summary of Inflammation and Cancer Think Tank," http://dcb.nci.nih.gov/thinktank thinktank/Executive_Summary_of_Inflammation_and _Cancer_Think_Tank.cfm (accessed March 12, 2010).
2. David Servan-Schreiber, *Anticancer: A New Way of Life* (New York: Viking, 2008), 40.
3. Jay Kimiecik quoted by Eric Harr, "Super Motivation from Superstar Athletes" blog, February 15, 2008, http://ericharr .wordpress.com/2008/02/ (accessed September 29, 2010); published in *Shape*, October 2003.
4. For more information about Bernie Siegel's resources, refer to www.ecap-online.org.
5. 1 Corinthians 9:24.
6. Barbara A. Elliott, "Forgiveness Therapy: A Clinical Intervention for Chronic Disease," *Journal of Religion and Health*, February 24, 2010. Several citations will refer to this online publication, which is without page numbers. The article can be ordered online through Springer Science+Business Media, LLC at www.SpringerLink.com.
7. 1 Corinthians 15:44.
8. James 4:13–15, emphasis added.
9. See Matthew 5:43–45.
10. Zechariah 4:6.
11. E-mail to the author, April 28, 2010.
12. Joshua D. Bishop, personal communication, February 2010.
13. Batool Ahadi and Saeed Ariapooran, "Role of Self and Other Forgiveness in Predicting Depression and Suicide Ideation of Divorcees," *Journal of Applied Sciences* 9, no. 19 (2009): 3598–601, http://scialert.net/abstract/?doi=jas.2009.3598.3601.
14. Elliott, "Forgiveness Therapy."
15. 1 Samuel 17:43.
16. You can read the full story in 1 Samuel 17.
17. Matthew 7:14.

Chapter 2 • Jayne

1. Jayne is correct in her general description of our dialogue. Because of the short periods of time in which I'm able to meet with patients (often only one or two days), conversations are often compressed into very short sessions, and occasionally I can come across a little less empathetic than I truly am. Words are important, and my use of them is chosen intentionally in order to diagnose concerns and treat them effectively, and, all too often, quickly.

Chapter 7 • The Biology of Stress

1. Harold Koenig, from his foreword in Michael S. Barry, *A Reason for Hope: Gaining Strength for Your Fight against Cancer* (Colorado Springs: Cook Communications, 2004), 13.
2. David Servan-Schreiber, *Anticancer: A New Way of Life* (New York: Viking, 2008), 141.
3. R. Elliot Willis, *Finding Grace on a Less Traveled Road* (New York: IUniverse, 2008), 174, 176.
4. Servan-Schreiber, *Anticancer* (2008), 146.
5. David Servan-Schreiber, *Anticancer: A New Way of Life* (New York: Viking, 2009), 175.
6. Barbara A. Elliott, "Forgiveness Therapy: A Clinical Intervention for Chronic Disease," *Journal of Religion and Health*, February 24, 2010. See note 6 of chapter 1.
7. Marilyn Elias, "Psychologists Now Know What Makes People Happy," *USA Today*, December 9, 2002), http://www.usatoday .com/news/health/2002-12-08-happy-main_x.htm (accessed May 16, 2010).
8. Beth Azar, "Father of PNI Reflects on the Field's Growth," *APA Monitor Online*, June 6, 1999, http://www.apa.org.
9. Ibid.
10. Robert M. Sapolsky, "The Physiology and Pathophysiology of Unhappiness," in *Handbook of Forgiveness*, ed. Everett L. Worthington Jr., (New York: Routledge, 2005), 278.

11. Psalm 139:13–14.
12. Robert Scaer, *The Trauma Spectrum: Hidden Wounds and Human Resiliency* (New York: Norton, 2005), 211.
13. Ibid., 252.
14. Charlotte vanOyen Witvliet, "Unforgiveness, Forgiveness, and Justice: Scientific Findings on Feelings and Physiology," in *Handbook of Forgiveness*, ed. Worthington, 312.
15. Jed Shlackman, "Research Links Cancer with Repressed, Unresolved Feelings and Emotions," blog, October 7, 2009, http://www.altmd.com/Specialists/Counseling-Hypnosis-Reiki-Holistic-Healing/Blog (accessed May 12, 2010).
16. Benson-Henry Institute for Mind Body Medicine, http://www.mgh.harvard.edu/bhi/about/ (accessed May 16, 2010).

Chapter 8 • Cancer and Emotional Trauma

1. Robert Scaer, *The Trauma Spectrum: Hidden Wounds and Human Resiliency* (New York: Norton, 2005), 246–47.
2. Dr. Braun's credentials in the field of immunology are noteworthy. Dr. Braun received his PhD in microbiology/immunology from the University of Illinois and has over thirty years of basic research experience in immunology, microbiology, and cell biology, as well as twenty-five years of clinical research experience in the areas of oncology, inflammatory diseases, and cancer immunotherapy. He is the former scientific director of the Rush Medical College Cancer Institute in Chicago, and the former administrative director of the Cancer Institute at the Medical College of Ohio, where he retains his academic appointment as a Volunteer Professor of Surgery in the basic science track. Dr. Braun has authored more than ninety published peer-reviewed manuscripts, twenty-three reviews and book chapters, and has coedited a textbook devoted to the use of prostaglandin inhibitors in cancer immunotherapy.
3. Donald P. Braun, video interview, Cancer Treatment Centers of America, Philadelphia, September 9, 2010.

4. Ibid.
5. Barbara A. Elliott, "Forgiveness Therapy: A Clinical Intervention for Chronic Disease," *Journal of Religion and Health*, February 24, 2010. See note 6 of chapter 1.
6. See Matthew 18.
7. Elliott, "Forgiveness Therapy."
8. Sura 42.
9. 1 John 4:20.
10. Keith J. Petrie, Roger J. Booth, and James W. Pennebaker, "The Immunological Effects of Thought Suppression," *Journal of Personality and Social Psychology* 75, no. 5 (1998): 1264.
11. Alex H. S. Harris and Carl E. Thoresen, "Forgiveness, Unforgiveness, Health, and Disease," *Handbook of Forgiveness*, ed. Everett L. Worthington Jr. (New York: Routledge, 2005), 323.
12. Scaer, *The Trauma Spectrum*, 209.
13. Christina M. Puchalski, "Forgiveness: Spiritual and Medical Implications," *The Yale Journal for Humanities in Medicine*, 2002, http://yjhm.yale.edu/archives/spirit2003/forgiveness/cpuchalski.htm (accessed May 16, 2010).
14. Ibid.
15. Lydia R. Temoshok and Rebecca L. Wald, "Forgiveness and Health in Persons with HIV/AIDS," in *Handbook of Forgiveness*, ed. Worthington, 341 (emphasis added).
16. Ibid., 344 (emphasis added).
17. Ibid., 325 (emphasis added).
18. S. E. Locke, abstract of "Emotional Disclosure Through Writing or Speaking Modulates Latent Epstein-Barr Virus Antibody Titers (B. A. Esterling, et. al.)," *Journal of Consulting and Clinical Psychology* 62, no. 1 (1994): 130–40.
19. Charlotte vanOyen Witvliet, "Unforgiveness, Forgiveness, and Justice: Scientific Findings on Feelings and Physiology," in *Handbook of Forgiveness*, ed. Worthington, 315.
20. What Doctors Don't Tell You, "The Psychology of Cancer," http://www.wddty.com/the-psychology-of-cancer.html (accessed May 12, 2010).

21. Edwin H. Friedman, *Friedman's Fables* (New York: Guilford, 1990), back matter discussion questions, 13.

Chapter 9 • In Search of Motivation
  1. Isaiah 55:8–9.
  2. ChangingMinds.org, Motivational Theories, http://changing minds.org/explanations/theories/a_motivation.htm (accessed May 16, 2010).
  3. Romans 7:18–19.
  4. Quotations Page, http://www.quotationspage.com/quote/3157 .html (accessed May 16, 2010).
  5. Mark 11:25.
  6. Matthew 6:14–15.
  7. C. S. Lewis, "On Forgiveness," in *The Weight of Glory: And Other Addresses* (New York: HarperCollins, 2001), 182.
  8. Romans 12:14.
  9. *The Mahabharata*, Vana Parva, section XXVII, translated by Sri Kisari Mohan Ganguli; http://www.hinduism.co.za /forgiven.htm.
  10. Galatians 5:19–21.
  11. Piero Ferrucci, *The Power of Kindness: The Unexpected Benefits of Leading a Compassionate Life* (New York: Tarcher/Penguin, 2006), 40 (italics in original).
  12. Maryjo Prince-Paul and Julie J. Exline, "Personal Relationship and Communication Messages at the End of Life," *Nursing Clinics of North America* 45, no. 3 (September 2010): 449–63.
  13. Matthew 28:20.

Chapter 10 • Debulking Forgiveness
  1. *The Mahabharata*, Udyoga Parva, section XXXIII, translated by Sri Kisari Mohan Ganguli; http://www.hinduism.co.za /forgiven.htm.
  2. John Patton, "Forgiveness in Pastoral Care and Counseling,"

in *Forgiveness: Theory, Research, and Practice*, ed., Michael E. McCullough, Kenneth I. Pargament, and Carl E. Thoresen (New York: Guilford, 2000), 283.

3. J. J. Exline, R. F. Baumeister, A. L. Zell, A. J. Kraft, and C. V. Witvliet, "Not So Innocent: Does Seeing One's Own Capacity for Wrongdoing Predict Forgiveness?" *Journal of Personal Social Psychology* 94, no. 3 (March 2008): 495–515.

4. James 4:17.

5. Speech by Robert F. Kennedy, "On the Mindless Menace of Violence," at the City Club of Cleveland, Ohio on April 5, 1968. For the full text, see http://rfkmemorial.mediathree.net /lifevision/onthemindlessmenaceofviolence.

6. Eli Malinsky, "A Culture of Forgiveness," Centre for Social Innovation blog, October 20, 2009, http://socialinnovation.ca /blog/culture-of-forgiveness.

7. Charles L. Griswold, *Forgiveness: A Philosophical Exploration* (Cambridge, MA: Cambridge University, 2007), xi.

8. Dream This Day Quotations, http://www.dreamthisday.com /forgiveness-quotes/ (accessed May 16, 2010).

9. Daniel Gilbert, *Stumbling on Happiness* (New York: Vintage Books, 2006), 198–99 (emphasis in original).

10. Matthew 18:22.

Chapter 11 • Release!

1. Merriam-Webster Online, s.v. *myth*, http://www.merriam -webster.com/dictionary/myth.

2. The Free Dictionary Online s.v., *reconcile*, http://www.thefree dictionary.com/reconcile.

3. Matthew 5:23–24.

4. Matthew 23:23.

5. Romans 12:19.

6. Romans 13:1–2.

7. Amos 5:24.

8. See Matthew 18:21–35.

9. Barbara A. Elliott, "Forgiveness Therapy: A Clinical Intervention for Chronic Disease," *Journal of Religion and Health*, February 24, 2010. See note 6 of chapter 1.

10. Andrée Seu, "The Thing We Don't Do," *World*, September 30, 2006, http://www.worldmag.com/articles/12263.

11. Regina Barreca, "Snow White Doesn't Live Here Anymore: Sweet Revenge," *Psychology Today*, January 1, 2010, http://www.webmd.com/balance/features/sweet-revenge.

12. John Roach, "Brain Study Shows Why Revenge Is Sweet," National Geographic News, http://news.nationalgeographic.com/news/2004/08/0827_040827_punishment.html; and Brian Knutson, "Sweet Revenge?" *Science* 305, no. 5688 (August 27, 2004): 1246–47, http://www.sciencemag.org.

13. John Calvin, *John*, ed. Alister McGrath and J. I. Packer, (Wheaton, IL: Crossway Books, 1994), 306.

14. Matthew 5:44.

15. Misty Harris, Virtue Online, "Prayer Boosts Forgiveness: Study," http://www.virtueonline.org/portal/modules/news/article.php?storyid=12487.

16. Robert Scaer, *The Trauma Spectrum: Hidden Wounds and Human Resiliency* (New York: Norton, 2005), 255.

17. Ibid., 68.

18. Ibid., 63.

19. Amanda Schaeffer, "Not a Game: Simulation to Lessen War Trauma," *New York Times*, August 28, 2007, http://www.nytimes.com/2007/08/28/health/28game.html?_r=1.

20. James Dao, "Simulators Prepare Soldiers for Explosions of War," *New York Times*, January 22, 2010, http://www.nytimes.com/2010/01/23/us/23simulator.html.

21. Keith J. Petrie, Roger J. Booth, and James W. Pennebaker, "The Immunological Effects of Thought Suppression," *Journal of Personality and Social Psychology* 75, no. 5 (1998): 1264.

22. Jane M. Richards, Wanda E. Beal, Janel D. Seagal, and James W. Pennebaker, "Effects of Disclosure of Traumatic Events on

Illness Behavior Among Psychiatric Prison Inmates," *Journal of Abnormal Psychology* 109, no. 1 (2000): 156.

23. James W. Pennebaker and Cindy K. Chung, "Expressive Writing and Its Links to Mental and Physical Health," *Oxford Handbook of Health Psychology*, ed. H. S. Friedman (New York: Oxford University Press, forthcoming); http://homepage.psy.utexas.edu/HomePage/Faculty/Pennebaker/Reprints/Pennebaker&Chung_FriedmanChapter.pdf (accessed May 16, 2010).

24. http://en.wikipedia.org/wiki/Huaorani.

25. Michael McCullough, *Beyond Revenge* (San Francisco: Jossey-Bass, 2008), 212.

26. Galatians 5:20.

Chapter 12 • Self-Forgiveness or Self-Acceptance?

1. Alan Jacobs, *Original Sin: A Cultural History* (New York: HarperOne, 2008), 26.

2. Justin Wheeler, "Paradoxes—A Puritan Prayer," blog, http://justinwheeler.wordpress.com/2010/02/11/paradoxes-a-puritan-prayer/ (accessed May 16, 2010).

3. The American Chesterton Society, http://chesterton.org/qmeister2/wrongtoday.htm.

4. Luke 18:9–14.

5. ThinkExist Quotations, http://thinkexist.com/quotation/when-you-make-a-mistake-don-t-look-back-at-it/1022852.html.

6. Lois C. Friedman, Catherine Romero, Richard Elledge, et al., "Attribution of Blame, Self-forgiving Attitude, and Psychological Adjustment in Women with Breast Cancer," *Journal of Behavioral Medicine* 30, no. 4 (August 2007): 351–57.

7. Lois C. Friedman, Catherine R. Barber, Jenny Chang, et al., "Self-blame, Self-forgiveness, and Spirituality in Breast Cancer Survivors in a Public Sector Setting," *Journal of Cancer Education* 25, no. 3 (September 2010).

8. L. A. Gerber, "Transformations in Self-understanding in Surgeons Whose Treatment Efforts Were Not Successful,"

American Journal of Psychotherapy 44, no. 1 (January 1990): 75–84.

9. J. G. Gonyea, R. Paris, and L. de Saxe Zerden, "Adult Daughters and Aging Mothers: The Role of Guilt in the Experience of Caregiver Burden," *Aging Mental Health* 12, no. 5 (September 2008): 559–67.

10. Paul C. Vitz and Jennifer M. Meade, "Self-forgiveness in Psychology and Psychotherapy: A Critique," *Journal of Religion and Health*, published online March 31, 2010.

11. Ibid.

12. Blue Letter Bible Lexicon, http://www.blueletterbible.org/lang /lexicon/lexicon.cfm?Strongs=G5461&t=KJV.

13. Psalm 18:28 NKJV.

14. Hebrews 6:4–6.

15. Proverbs 2:6.

16. 2 Samuel 11–12.

17. Luke 23:34.

18. Exodus 20:5.

19. Vitz and Meade, "Self-forgiveness in Psychology."

20. Ibid.

21. Michael E. McCullough, Kenneth I. Pargament, and Carl E. Thoresen, *Forgiveness: Theory, Research and Practice* (New York: Guilford, 2000), 164–65.

22. Acts 8:1.

23. Vitz and Meade, "Self-forgiveness in Psychology."

24. 1 Samuel 13:14.

25. Mark Shaw, *Beneath the Mask of Holiness* (New York: Palgrave MacMillan, 2009), 177.

26. Emphasis added.

27. R. C. Sproul, "Is the Church Full of Hypocrites?" *TableTalk Magazine*, October 2009, http://www.ligonier.org/learn /articles/church-full-hypocrites/ (accessed May 12, 2010).

28. Preface by Gordon W. Allport, in Viktor E. Frankl, *Man's Search for Meaning* (Boston: Beacon, 1992), 7.

29. Frankl, *Man's Search for Meaning*, 10.

30. 2 Corinthians 5:10.
31. Acts 26:20.
32. John 8:32.
33. 1 John 1:9.
34. Matthew 18:35.
35. Micah 6:8.
36. 2 Corinthians 12:7b–10.

Conclusion • Cool Quickly
1. Psalm 41:9.

Epilogue • Eva's Story
1. Eva's story has been reprinted from Margo O'Hara, "Surviving the Angel of Death," Gapers Block, February 27, 2010, http://gapersblock.com/ac/2010/02/27/surviving-the-angel-of-death/. Reprinted with permission of the author and Gapers Block.
2. Some estimates of people killed at Auschwitz during World War II exceed 1 million. It's possible that O'Hara meant 700,000 here.
3. Dr. Munch was an SS physician at Auschwitz. He was the only person acquitted at the Auschwitz trials, and was reportedly responsible for saving the lives of many Jews.

Assistance in Healthcare

Assistance in Healthcare, Inc. (AIH) is a nonprofit charitable organization dedicated to helping cancer patients who are undergoing treatment in the local Philadelphia area, and their families, by lessening the financial burden of cancer. Because medical expenses can make the road to recovery far more difficult, the foundation attempts to pave the way by providing assistance to those who have become financially distressed as a result of their courageous fight. We do this by donating grants to help defray the costs of nonmedical needs such as utilities, housing, transportation, and basic living expenses to eligible patients or their immediate family members so that patients can focus on what's important—their healing.

Michael S. Barry (DMin, Fuller Theological Seminary; MA, Princeton Theological Seminary) is Director of Pastoral Care at Cancer Treatment Centers of America in Philadelphia, where he specializes in the connection between spirituality and health. He has served in the ministry for over twenty years and has appeared on numerous radio and television shows around the country. He is the author of *A Reason for Hope*, *A Season for Hope*, and *The Art of Caregiving*.